Praying for you!
Jaël Naomie
5·2020

Jaëlnaomie16 @ gmail.com

One Minute with God

with

Devotional Prayer Journal

Jaël Naomie

WESTBOW
PRESS®
A DIVISION OF THOMAS NELSON
& ZONDERVAN

WestBow Press books may be ordered through booksellers or by contacting:

WestBow Press
A Division of Thomas Nelson & Zondervan
1663 Liberty Drive
Bloomington, IN 47403
www.westbowpress.com
1 (866) 928-1240

ISBN: 978-1-5127-9323-9 (sc)
ISBN: 978-1-5127-9324-6 (hc)
ISBN: 978-1-5127-9322-2 (e)

Library of Congress Control Number: 2017910603

Printed in the United States of America.

WestBow Press rev. date: 8/10/2017

To June Powel—Thank you for praying with me every morning. Your prayers will be missed, but pray I will.

To Andrew O. Gordon, Orville Bailey, and Stephen J. Francis—Thank you for the constant love and encouragement. Keep 'em coming.

To Esdras, Theodore, Judith, and Mom—A family bond that is unbreakable!

January 1

At the time appointed ...

—Genesis 18:14 (KJV)

But like the stars in the vast circuit of their appointed path, God's purposes know no haste and no delay. (DA 32.1)

*O*h my God, we can learn so much from you about your divine nature, your attributes, your love, and your character. As your sons and daughters, we desire to have an intimate relationship with you. This year, we want a closer walk with you so we can learn more about you and know you more intimately. We give you thanks for Christ, who dwells in us by the power of your Holy Spirit. We wholly trust that at the appointed time, your will for our lives, your children, will be done and you will be glorified. We pray in the holy name of Jesus, amen.

Reflections, Thoughts, and Prayers

_____

_____

_____

_____

_____

_____

January 2

The LORD is my shepherd: I shall not want.
—Psalm 23:1 (KJV)

When we think of a shepherd, we think of someone who cares for the flock. So it is with Christ; He is the Good Shepherd. He is ever looking to do us good. He protects our comings and goings. He looks for ways to bless us. He never sleeps or slumbers. His constant gaze is on us, His beloved children. We can rest assured all our provisions have been made—we shall want for nothing.

Heavenly Father, why do we doubt your goodness and love? Today, I ask for forgiveness and I surrender this heart to you. You have provided and met all my needs, and I know I will want for nothing because you are the Good Shepherd in whom I trust, amen.

Reflections, Thoughts, and Prayers

_____

_____

_____

_____

_____

_____

_____

January 3

Trust in the LORD with all thine heart: and
lean not unto thine own understanding.
—Proverbs 3:5 (KJV)

To trust means to have a firm belief in the reliability of a person. Here, you are being asked to trust in the Lord with all your heart. You have to learn to trust your heavenly Father.

At times in our lives, we worry about things that may never come to pass. We waste precious moments worrying when we could have been enjoying our lives. God wants us to trust Him. He wants us to know He is willing and able to help. He bids us look at how He has led us in the past, and He wants us to trust He is leading even now.

Heavenly Father, we come to you because you are our all in all. May we trust you and know that no good thing will you keep from us. Even when we can't understand what's happening in our lives, help us trust in you today and forever, amen.

Reflections, Thoughts, and Prayers

_____

_____

_____

_____

_____

_____

January 4

But let him ask in faith, nothing wavering.
—James 1:6 (KJV)

Long delays tire the angels. It is even more excusable to make a wrong decision sometimes than to be continually in a wavering position, to be hesitating, sometimes inclined in one direction then in another. More perplexity and doubting than from sometimes moving too hastily. (GW 133.4)

*H*eavenly Father, as the year is fresh and new, we pray we will make haste through every door you open. May we cultivate a relationship with you so we will know your way and your voice. We pray for that childlike faith—with nothing wavering, believing you are able. Increase our faith and love for you. We pray this in Jesus's name, amen.

Reflections, Thoughts, and Prayers

_____

_____

_____

_____

_____

_____

January 5

So run, that ye may obtain.
—1 Corinthians 9:24 (KJV)

*W*e are not to be idle as if sitting and expecting great blessings to fall into our laps. We are to run so we may obtain. Jesus expected much, so He attempted much. Should we not follow His example? Be active in your life. You're your faith.

Oh my God, who is in heaven, we pray for an active lifestyle in reaching others for you and in building the character that will prepare us for heaven. Help us never to lose the boldness to stay active in your cause and represent you in all circumstances. May we walk with the assurance that you, the God of Abraham, Isaac, and Israel, walks with us. Help us pursue the desires you have placed in our hearts knowing we have nothing to lose. We pray this in Jesus's name, amen.

Reflections, Thoughts, and Prayers

_____

_____

_____

_____

_____

_____

January 6

And God said … and it was so.
—Genesis 1:9 (KJV)

What can the angels of heaven think of poor helpless human beings, who are subject to temptation, when God's heart of infinite love yearns toward them, ready to give them more than they can ask or think, and yet they pray so little and have so little faith? (SC94).

*H*eavenly Father, it is clear in your Word that what you speak comes to pass and what you have promised to do you will do. Take away our complaining and our doubts. Increase our faith as we develop the habit to pray. This is our prayer in Jesus's name, amen.

Reflections, Thoughts, and Prayers

_____

_____

_____

_____

_____

_____

_____

January 7

I will be with thee.
—Joshua 3:7 (KJV)

*T*his is such an assuring promise the Lord of our lives has made to those who are called by His name. No matter where you may find yourself, know that God is with you. No matter what you may be going through, know that God is with you. If you can feel His presence in the best of times, look for Him in the worst of times—because He is there. As He was with Moses and Joshua, so He is now with you.

Loving Father, we ask you to motivate us to work for you so we can reach others right where you have placed us. Help us trust you are with us always even unto the end. Give us a desire to seek the lost. We pray this for Christ's sake, amen.

Reflections, Thoughts, and Prayers

_____

_____

_____

_____

_____

_____

_____

_____

January 8

And he marveled because of their unbelief.
—Mark 6:6 (KJV)

The secret of all failures is our failure in secret prayer.
(KC 14)

*H*eavenly Father, we all would say we believe in prayer, but do we truly believe in the power of prayer? Do we even take the time to pray? Help us by the power of your Holy Spirit to prevail in prayer. May we PUSH (Pray Until Something Happens) because we pray to the one and only true and wise God! Amen.

Reflections, Thoughts, and Prayers

_____

_____

_____

_____

_____

_____

_____

_____

January 9

Men ought always to pray, and not to faint.
—Luke 18:1 (KJV)

It is not too much to say that all real growth in the spiritual life-all victory over temptation, all confidence and peace in the presence of difficulties and dangers, all repose of spirit in times of great disappointment or loss, all habitual communion with God- depends upon the practice of secret prayer. (KC 9)

Heavenly Father, my heart's desire is to know you. Here I stand in the battlefield asking you to be my guide—because without you, I will surely perish. Do for your children what only you can do. I pray for Christ's sake, amen.

Reflections, Thoughts, and Prayers

_____

_____

_____

_____

_____

_____

_____

January 10

For in him we live, and move, and have our being.
—Acts 17:28 (KJV)

The hand of infinite power is perpetually at work guiding this planet. It is God's power momentarily exercised that keeps it in position in its rotations. The God of heaven is constantly at work. It is by His power that vegetation is caused to flourish, that every leaf appears and every flower blooms. Every breath, every throb of the heart, is the continual evidence of the power of an ever-present God. (6BC 1062.5)

*O*h, my God, when we consider your awesomeness, we have no need to wallow in fear or worry because everything that we are we are because of you. We give you thanks, amen.

Reflections, Thoughts, and Prayers

_____

_____

_____

_____

_____

_____

January 11

Ask, and ye shall receive, that your joy may be full.
—John 16:24 (KJV)

*D*on't limit God with your unbelief. Make your request and you will receive. It's that simple. God is waiting on you. Go on, ask.

Heavenly Father, our greatest need is you! And we have access to you through prayer. Loving Dad, we pray we may know what your will for our lives is. Thank you for reminding us that our joy depends on answered prayer. May we shake off the lethargy by the power of your Holy Spirit, and let us ask so we may receive so we may be joyful, amen.

Reflections, Thoughts, and Prayers

_____

_____

_____

_____

_____

_____

_____

_____

_____

January 12

If my people, which are called by my name, shall
humble themselves, and pray, and seek my face, and turn
from their wicked ways; then will I hear from heaven,
and will forgive their sin, and will heal their land.
—2 Chronicles 7:14 (KJV)

When I became an adult and still had some amazing dreams to accomplish, the one and only gift I would ask of others was the gift of prayer. But I wouldn't ask just anyone; I would ask the people I knew who prayed—those who believed in the power of prayer—to pray for me. There is no greater gift than the gift of prayer.

Heavenly Father, you have given to us, your children, the recipe for a connection with you and all you represent—humility, prayer, and change. May we take heed and humble ourselves, and may we pray so we may be healed physically, mentally, and spiritually in Jesus's name, amen.

Reflections, Thoughts, and Prayers

_____

_____

_____

_____

_____

_____

January 13

I believe God ...
—Acts 27:25 (KJV)

*I*t is important to know who God is and develop a relationship with Him. If you don't know God, you won't understand His movements.

Loving Father who art in heaven, if I am going to follow you wherever you lead, I need to believe in you. Abraham believed in you so much that when you asked him to leave his relatives and home and go to a strange land, he trusted and followed you. We come in prayer and in faith. Like Abraham, may we believe you and know it will be just as you have said. We want to know you. For if we know you, we won't doubt you, amen.

Reflections, Thoughts, and Prayer

_____

_____

_____

_____

_____

_____

_____

_____

> And being not weak in faith, he considered not his
> own body now dead, when he was about an hundred
> years old, neither yet the deadness of Sarah's womb:
> He staggered not at the promise of God through
> unbelief; but was strong in faith, giving glory to God.
> —Romans 4:19–20 (KJV)

God knows how to take us to a place where all heaven and earth will know we know who God is, and if He says it, He will do it. I know if I were Abraham, my faith would have grown cold because in the natural, it doesn't seem to be possible to have a child when everything in me is dead. But God invites us to "taste and see that the Lord is good" (Psalm 34:8), and what He has promised, He will do.

Yes, Father, you are on the throne and are working miracles in the lives of your children who believe. You did it in the life of Abraham, and you can do the impossible for us. May our eyes stay on you and not on our circumstances we pray, amen.

Reflections, Thoughts, and Prayer

_____

_____

_____

_____

_____

January 15

He believed in the LORD.
—Genesis 15:6 (KJV)

*O*ur lives should have a plethora of blessings displaying God's work in our lives. As His children, we have the evidence to rest our faith in His loving arms. There is no room for doubt when it is so clear God is with us, and all nations will call you blessed.

Heavenly Father, your Word is clear. We need to take you at your word. We need to believe. Let us meditate on how you have led us in the past so our faith may be strengthened, and like Abraham, may it be said of us that we believed the Lord, amen.

Reflections, Thoughts, and Prayer

_____

_____

_____

_____

_____

_____

_____

_____

January 16

And being fully persuaded that, what he had
promised, he was able also to perform.
—Romans 4:21 (KJV)

Have there not been some bright spots in your
experience? Have you not had some precious seasons
when your heart throbbed with joy in response to the
Spirit of God? When you look back into the chapters
of your life experience do you not find some pleasant
pages? Are not God's promises, like the fragrant flowers,
growing beside your path on every hand? Will you not
let their beauty and sweetness fill your heart with joy?
(SC 117.1)

L oving Father, may we be fully persuaded that you will perform
what you have promised. Take away all discouragements and
gloom, and give us your joy we pray in Jesus's name, amen.

Reflections, Thoughts, and Prayer

_____

_____

_____

_____

_____

_____

January 17

Is any thing too hard for the LORD?
—Genesis 18:14 (KJV)

God loves to do the impossible. He loves to work in such a way that when the work is done, you have zero doubt that it was God. Just look at how He parted the Red Sea when the children of Israel were thinking they were doomed because they couldn't see the way out. When it seems impossible, that's the time to call on your heavenly Father, the God of the impossible.

Forgive me, Father, for I have been guilty of uttering such doubts. I pray my words and actions never put you to shame. Increase my faith so I too will see all the blessings you have in store for me to come my way. Increase my faith I pray in Jesus's name, amen.

Reflections, Thoughts, and Prayer

_____

_____

_____

_____

_____

_____

_____

January 18

And she named the child I-chabod, saying,
The glory is departed from Israel.
—1 Samuel 4:21 (KJV)

*I*t is not a good idea to dwell on the disappointments of life and fixate on all the unpleasant things that have occurred. That will bring about a downcast, overwhelmed spirit. Instead, let us talk of the goodness of the Lord and all the wonderful things He has done.

Loving Father, we know we make mistakes, but we also know you are a forgiving God. Let us not be like Ichabod's mother and name our future based on our past mistakes. May we look to Jesus always and know that our futures are bright because He is in it. It is in His name that we move forward embracing our futures, amen.

Reflections, Thoughts, and Prayer

_____

_____

_____

_____

_____

_____

_____

January 19

Yet as soon as the priests who carried the ark
reached the Jordan and their feet touched the water's
edge, the water from upstream stopped flowing.
It piled up in a heap a great distance away.
—Joshua 3:15–16 (NIV)

One of the most essential qualities of the faith that is to attempt great things for God, and expect great things from God, is holy audacity. Where we are dealing with a supernatural Being, and taking from Him things that are humanly impossible, it is easier to take much than little; it is easier to stand in a place of audacious trust than in a place of cautious, timid clinging to the shore. (SD 3/28).

L oving Father, may we attempt great things for you. Take away the timid, cautious attitude and give us that holy audacity to do great and expect great today and every day, amen.

Reflections, Thoughts, and Prayer

January 20

And whatsoever ye shall ask in my name, that will
I do, that the Father may be glorified in the Son. If
ye shall ask any thing in my name I will do it.
—John 14:13–14 (KJV)

*L*earn how to persevere in prayer and press your request to our Father, who's in heaven, in the name of Jesus. God will honor that name.

Heavenly Father, your Word is clear. You will do anything we ask for. We pray to know what we ought to pray for so we may glorify you, our Father. May we press our petitions to heaven for lost souls and opportunities to witness for you. We know you will fill all we lack. We pray in the matchless name of Jesus, amen.

Reflections, Thoughts, and Prayer

_____

_____

_____

_____

_____

_____

_____

January 21

Hold your peace.
—Job 13:13 (KJV)

*W*e talk way too much about the things that perplex us and praise God way too little for all the good He has done. We need to keep in mind that heaven is constantly in our midst. The angels are grieved when all we do is murmur and complain about our situations making no mention of God and His greatness.

God knows how to work behind the scenes. He sees what no eyes can see. Let us learn to hold our peace when trials cross our paths. Let us learn to pray giving God thanks for all His goodness.

Heavenly Father, I want to realize you are in my midst no matter where I am and whom I am with. I ask your Holy Spirit to bring to my remembrance that I need to be careful what I say and how I say it because I don't want to grieve the heavenly beings. Help me hold my peace I pray in Jesus's name, amen.

Reflections, Thoughts, and Prayer

_____

_____

_____

_____

_____

January 22

Watch ye therefore, and pray always, that ye may be
accounted worthy to escape all these things that shall
come to pass, and to stand before the Son of man.
—Luke 21:36 (KJV)

Many attend religious services and come out no better than when they entered. They continue to gossip, murmur, and complain about God or each other. One of the biggest reasons for this is a lack of prayer in their lives. Prayer changes things. Prayer changes people. When the darkness and sufferings of the mind set in, we have only ourselves to blame for not studying, watching, and praying. We need to pray in everything for everything. Let us pray!

Heavenly Father, may we take time to meditate on your holy Word and pray even if it is one minute before beginning our day so we may have the strength to stand these last days. We pray in Jesus's name, amen.

Reflections, Thoughts, and Prayer

_____

_____

_____

_____

_____

_____

January 23

The fear of the LORD is the beginning of wisdom:
and the knowledge of the holy is understanding.
—Proverbs 9:10 (KJV)

*K*nowing God is the foundation of all true education. This should be the goal of every home, church, school, and community. This doesn't apply only to the little ones but to us all as well. We need to pray for a character that will reflect Christ. Even if parents or leaders didn't provide you a solid foundation for character building, it is not too late to come to Jesus. He will make you into a new creature. Jesus is standing at the door of your heart and is knocking. Won't you open the door so He may come in?

Loving Father, this morning, we come because we need wisdom to distinguish between the holy and the profane. We need a cleaning starting from our inside on out. We need Jesus. We come because we want a powerful prayer life. Please show us whatever is hindering your power when we pray so we might cooperate with your Holy Spirit to change and reflect more of your character. We pray this in Jesus's name, amen.

Reflections, Thoughts, and Prayers

_____

_____

_____

_____

_____

January 24

And it shall be said in that day, Lo, this is our God;
we have waited for him, and he will save us.
—Isaiah 25:9 (KJV)

We have waited a long time, and we have but a short while to wait before Jesus will descend from heaven to take us home. The prophecies are quickly being fulfilled. Now is the time to study, pray, and prepare. The mighty and glorious day is fast approaching when the dead in Christ will be awakened from their sleeping graves by He who holds the keys to the grave and be caught up with those who never experienced death. We will shout "Alleluia" and worship the Lamb forever. Stay faithful, friends!

Redeemer of all created beings, what a day it will be when you come back to take us home. I pray you will keep me faithful until that great day now and forever, amen.

Reflections, Thoughts, and Prayer

_____

_____

_____

_____

_____

_____

January 25

And I John saw the holy city, New Jerusalem.
—Revelation 21:2 (KJV)

This temple was supported by seven pillars, all of transparent gold, set with pearls most glorious. The wonderful things I there saw I cannot describe. Oh, that I could talk in the language of Canaan, then could I tell a little of the glory of the better world. Soon we heard Jesus' lovely voice again, saying, "Come, My people, you have come out of great tribulation, and done My will; suffered for Me; come in to supper, for I will gird Myself, and serve you." We shouted, "Alleluia! glory!" and entered into the city. (EW 19.1)

*H*eavenly Father, I desire to make it into that city paved of gold. I give thanks for Jesus, who has made it possible by the shedding of His blood. I pray your Holy Spirit will daily work in me to build my character to reflect yours, amen.

Reflections, Thoughts, and Prayer

_____

_____

_____

_____

_____

January 26

> For all people will walk every one in the name
> of his god, and we will walk in the name of
> the LORD our God forever and ever.
> —Micah 4:5 (KJV)

*J*esus said, "My yoke is easy, my burden is light" (Matthew 11:30). Let us learn to follow His leading so we may experience a lighter load. He can make the rough roads smooth and the crooked roads straight. He is waiting to make life more joyful and take our heavy trials. But we must be willing to follow His leading and trust Him.

I thank you, Father, for loving me so much that you have made provisions for every emergency. Lord, it is my desire to make it to heaven. I ask forgiveness for my sins, and I accept your forgiveness in Jesus's name, amen.

Reflections, Thoughts, and Prayer

_____

_____

_____

_____

_____

_____

_____

January 27

Strive to enter in at the strait gate: for many, I say unto
you, will seek to enter in, and shall not be able.
—Luke 13:24 (KJV)

*S*atan is actively seeking to see whom he may devour, and we must
be active too in thought, action, and prayer. There is heaven to gain.
We are no match for the enemy of the soul, but Jesus is. We are to strive
to be hid in Christ so He will fight every battle for us. When we are in
Christ, we are more than conquerors.

There is no time for blaming others for where we are in our spiritual
walk with God. The excuse time has ended. The acting time to seek
Jesus and stay in His presence has begun. It is a lifelong work.

Heavenly Father, you have given us your only begotten Son, who
has made it possible for all who are willing to be saved. I pray many will
strive to enter the straight gate. It may be bumpy and full of trials but
only for a season because Jesus has overcome the world, amen.

Reflections, Thoughts, and Prayer

_____

_____

_____

_____

_____

January 28

All scripture is given by inspiration of God,
and is profitable for doctrine, for reproof, for
correction, for instruction in righteousness.
—2 Timothy 3:16 (KJV)

Those who know their weaknesses in conduct, habits, and practices are to go to the Word for correction and instructions on how to be more like Christ. Those who are not sure of their weaknesses are to go to the Word for reproof. As you take time to study, Jesus will reveal Himself more and more to you. The Holy Scripture is given for our use to grow and reflect the love of Jesus. God wants to mold and polish us until His original image of Himself is restored in us.

Heavenly Father, thank you for your inspired Word, a roadmap to your heavenly kingdom where we can come boldly to chat with you. Continue to help us grow in spirit and in truth. I pray in Jesus's name, amen.

Reflections, Thoughts, and Prayer

_____

_____

_____

_____

_____

_____

January 29

But we all, with open face beholding as in a glass the
glory of the Lord, are changed into the same image
from glory to glory, even as by the Spirit of the Lord.
—2 Corinthians 3:18 (KJV)

*I*n the beginning was the Word. Jesus is the Word you need to behold daily so you might grow more like Him. In knowing Christ, you will find the strength to endure life's little annoyances. The inner life will be strong, and the outer life will conform more to the will of God. This is a work we can do as we cooperate with His Holy Spirit.

Heavenly Father, you created us in your image, and I pray that by your Holy Spirit we will one day reflect your image fully once more. I pray we will make better choices in what we choose to watch and listen to, the places we choose to go, and the people we choose to associate with so as we behold you, we may become more like you. I pray in Jesus's name, amen.

Reflections, Thoughts, and Prayer

_____

_____

_____

_____

_____

_____

January 30

My tongue also shall talk of thy righteousness
all the daylong.
—Psalm 71:24 (KJV)

Human agents naturally love to complain. Nine good things may happen, which should be enough to give God the praise, but we fixate on the one bad thing that happened and miss out on enjoying the other nine. Let's cultivate the habit of being grateful.

The fictitious Pollyanna was a very positive girl. If she broke her left foot, instead of fixating on the broken foot, she would give thanks that her right foot wasn't broken because she hopped better on the right one anyway. Pollyanna would always look at the bright side of things. No matter what is happening, just remember all things are working out for your good because you are God's child. That is enough to speak of His goodness all the day long.

One day, every tongue will confess you are God and bow down in adoration, but I want that day to start today with my praise and thanksgiving talking of your great love for Christ's sake, amen.

Reflections, Thoughts, and Prayer

_____

_____

_____

_____

January 31

But when the righteous turneth away from his
righteousness, and committeth iniquity, and
doeth according to all the abominations that
the wicked man doeth, shall he live?
—Ezekiel 18:24 (KJV)

In fact, it can easily be shown that all want of success
and all failure in the spiritual life and in Christian work
is due to defective or insufficient prayer. Unless we pray
aright we cannot live aright or serve aright. Our Savior's
three great commands for definite action were –Pray
ye, -Do this, and –Go ye. It is our duty to pray so that
we might stand. (KC16)

*L*oving Father, we thank you for the invitation to leave the world
with its idols and follow in your way. We accept and ask for the
infilling of your Holy Spirit to come and cleanse us in Jesus's name,
amen.

Reflections, Thoughts, and Prayer

_____

_____

_____

_____

_____

February 1

Therefore I will give thanks unto thee, O LORD, among
the heathen, and I will sing praises unto thy name.
—2 Samuel 22:50 (KJV)

*Y*our devotional exercises should begin with praising God. Give God thanks for His grace. Give God thanks for His mercy. Give God thanks for His love. Praise Him for His strength. Praise God for His abundance. Praise God for His beauty. It isn't enough to present our wants and never take time to praise Him for what He has given us. Take time to give Him thanks. Take time to show your gratitude.

Heavenly Father, you are faithful, and all the world needs to know just how good, just, kind, and loving you are. I want to sing your praises among the nations. May your great name be exalted throughout the world I pray with thanksgiving in Jesus's name, amen.

Reflections, Thoughts, and Prayer

_____

_____

_____

_____

_____

_____

_____

February 2

Whoso offereth praise glorifieth me.
—Psalm 50:23 (KJV)

L et us cultivate the habit of praising God in all things and at all times. The Lord desires us to make mention of His great love for us and tell others of His power. He is honored by our praises and is delighted when we are thankful for all He is doing. God desires that the whole life of His children should be a life of praise.

Heavenly Father, we praise you today because you have loved us with such love that no human mind can know its full extent—more than all the grains of sand or stars above. You have withheld nothing to buy us back from the pit of darkness. You've given us your only begotten Son, Jesus, to show us you would give all you have for us because we matter. I pray that daily our lives will glorify you; I pray that daily we will sing your praises. Until that day where we may sing with all the angels and all the redeemed, we pray in Jesus's name, amen.

Reflections, Thoughts, and Prayer

_____

_____

_____

_____

_____

February 3

Ye are my witnesses, saith the LORD, that I am God.
—Isaiah 43:12 (KJV)

God is counting on us to show the world He is who He says He is. How are you representing God? Do you talk of His goodness, or do you complain when the slightest little thing goes wrong? Do you walk in obedience before Him, or do you do as you please but still say you are a follower of the Living God? Do you serve Him with life, joy, and gladness, or are you one of those whose life has been sapped out and now all hope is gone? Do you point others to Jesus by the way you live? How are you representing God?

Heavenly Father, you are worthy of our praises. Help me do a better job of representing you to the world. So many are turning to alcohol and drugs because they have not become acquainted with their wonderful Redeemer, who gave His life so all might have life. How wonderful it is to know Christ, amen.

Reflections, Thoughts, and Prayer

_____

_____

_____

_____

_____

February 4

I am but a little child: I know not
how to go out or come in.
—1 Kings 3:7 (KJV)

*W*hat a precious sight to see—children whose trust is in their fathers, children who believe their fathers are capable of making everything happen. So it ought to be with our heavenly Father and us. Our lips should express by prayer and praise our love and fondness of our heavenly Father so all may know we worship God in simplicity, truth, and the beauty of holiness. Let those who claim to be His children awaken to their responsibility.

Creator of all, we adore you and lift up your holy name with praise and thanksgiving. We thank you for your protection even in the battles of life. We thank you for recognizing that the warrior is a child, and we have total dependence on you. May our praises and songs be heard from one mountaintop to another until the whole world knows you are God and God alone, amen.

Reflections, Thoughts, and Prayer

_____

_____

_____

_____

_____

_____

February 5

If there be any praise, think on these things.
—Philippians 4:8 (KJV)

Our enemies may appear to have the victory. They may speak harsh words of deceit, accusation, and scam, yet we will stand and not be moved. We know God is still on the throne and sees every little teardrop we cry, every little heartache in us. We know in whom we believe. A day is coming when all wrong will be made right. Keep looking to the lovely things God has created for your enjoyment, and meditate on His goodness. The world is dark; trials may be at every turn, yet for all this, we will not be moved; we will lean on the arm of the mighty One for strength.

We lean on you, our mighty God, Father, and Friend because we know you have already won the war between good and evil. This morning, we pray you will keep our minds on you and the lovely things of heaven. No matter what our circumstances may be, may praise and gladness fill our hearts. We ask this in Jesus's name, amen.

Reflections, Thoughts, and Prayers

February 6

And he saith unto them, Follow me, and
I will make you fishers of men.
—Matthew 4:19 (KJV)

One of the most rewarding things we can do is serve others. Though this world is filled with sin and all uncouth things, when we learn to serve others, our hearts become full of joy and purpose. Selfish people do not experience such gladness. It is in service that we find our greatest joy and our highest education, "the riches of the glory of this mystery," "which is Christ in you, the hope of glory" (Colossians 1:27).

Loving Father, we praise you for the many blessings you have given us. We want to reach the world and tell everyone of your goodness. Let all come so they may see how good you are. Empower us by your Holy Spirit to live lives that will draw all humanity to you. We ask this in Jesus's name, amen.

Reflections, Thoughts, and Prayer

_____

_____

_____

_____

_____

_____

February 7

> Then said I, Here am I; send me.
> —Isaiah 6:8 (KJV)

God uses those who make themselves available for service. When heaven and earth unite to work together, we can have an experience similar to the one the apostles experienced on the Day of Pentecost. One may plant, another may water, and another may prune, but the increase comes from God. Humanity cannot accomplish what only God can. Make yourself available for His service.

Heavenly Father, we praise you because you are awesome, majestic, and true. Only a Father as loving as you would invite humanity in the state and condition we are in to come and work alongside you. Father, I desire to be used by you. Here I am, Lord—send me. I know you will multiply my efforts and bring about many blessings because it is all about you, amen.

Reflections, Thoughts, and Prayer

_____

_____

_____

_____

_____

_____

February 8

Can two walk together, except they be agreed?
—Amos 3:3 (KJV)

*N*o one is worth your losing heaven. Think long and hard before saying, "I do!" Many long for the day when they will wed, but it is truly a decision that will affect you on earth and in the life after. Think of what your home will be like when it is time for daily family worship. Will your spouse be supportive when it is time to pray? Don't rush into the matter. Pray about all things; God will show you the way.

Heavenly Father, the enemy is attacking homes and the institution of marriage between a man and a woman as you created it. I pray for families everywhere who are trying to live honorable lives that are pleasing to you. Help them grow in your love and live lives that follow the example of Jesus for His name's sake, amen.

Reflections, Thoughts, and Prayer

_____

_____

_____

_____

_____

_____

_____

February 9

When I consider thy heavens, the work of thy fingers,
the moon and the stars, which thou hast ordained.
—Psalm 8:3 (KJV)

G od loves all beautiful things. Everything God created is good. When we study nature and all the lush, colorful scenery that surrounds us, we will see how great God's heart must be. If we count every snowflake, every grain of sand in every corner of the world, every star in the universe, God's love for us is still greater than that.

Heavenly Father, nature testifies of you and your love for humanity. Help us enjoy the natural things of this world and give you thanks along the way. We pray this in Jesus's name, amen.

Reflections, Thoughts, and Prayer

_____

_____

_____

_____

_____

_____

_____

February 10

Study to shew thyself approved unto God, a
workman that needeth not to be ashamed,
rightly dividing the word of truth.
—2 Timothy 2:15 (KJV)

Our faith, our example, must be held more sacred than they have been held in the past. The word of God must be studied as never before; for it is the precious offering that we must present to men, in order that they may learn the way of peace, and obtain that life which measures with the life of God. Human wisdom so highly exalted among men sinks into insignificance before that wisdom which points out the way cast up for the ransomed of the Lord to walk in. (The Review *and Herald*, December 15, 1891).

*H*eavenly Father, I am in need of you today. Help me meditate today on your mercy and grace and give thanks to you for everything I have. Without you, I can do nothing. I pray for your Holy Spirit to keep me faithful today in Jesus's name, amen.

Reflections, Thoughts, and Prayer

_____

_____

_____

_____

_____

February 11

> Hide me from the conspiracy of the wicked,
> from that noisy crowd of evildoers.
> —Psalm 64:2 (NIV)

The enemy works tirelessly to sow discord, discouragement, and distrust among God's people. We focus the energy on our loved ones when we should be on our knees lifting up the name of Jesus and the one being used by the power of darkness.

Heavenly Father, I pray for the Holy Spirit to direct my thinking. I want to meditate on the life of Jesus Christ, who died for me on Calvary. I want to be hid in Christ and to focus on the blessings, not what others may say about or think of me. Help me run my race so one day I may hear from your holy throne room, "This is my child in whom I am well pleased."

Reflections, Thoughts, and Prayer

_____

_____

_____

_____

_____

_____

_____

February 12

How then can I do this great wickedness,
and sin against God?
—Genesis 39:9 (KJV)

*D*oes Jesus feel the nails every time we sin? We need to ponder the great sacrifice Jesus made to reconnect humanity to our heavenly Father. It would do our soul good to spend an hour meditating on the love of God. Only when our relationship deepens with our Creator will we stop indulging in sin. Sin would not be so lightly regarded if our eyes stayed fixed on the Redeemer of the world. Our words, manners, and habits would show we are children of a loving Lord. We need to abide in Christ so we may get the nutrients we need to grow.

Heavenly Father, I ask for your forgiveness from my sins, and I ask for victory over all cherished sin in Jesus's name, amen.

Reflections, Thoughts, and Prayer

_____

_____

_____

_____

_____

_____

_____

February 13

God forbid that I should sin against the
LORD in ceasing to pray for you.
—1 Samuel 12:23 (KJV)

How well do we know the difficulties that surround the prayer life of many? We are asked to pray one for another because we do not know what someone may be going through that prevents him or her from praying.

I encourage those who seem unable to get solitude at all to pray; I encourage them to make that a matter of prayer. As others lift you up in prayer, be sure to gain from the strength until you are able to develop a prayer life for yourself.

Heavenly Father, I pray today for all my family, friends, and loved ones. I pray for our leaders and pastors to look to you for guidance. And Lord, I pray you remember me today, amen.

Reflections, Thoughts, and Prayer

_____

_____

_____

_____

_____

_____

February 14

And I will call on the name of the LORD.
—1 Kings 18:24 (KJV)

God desires us to trust in Him. Come to His throne with boldness trusting that He is able and willing to give you what you seek. Jesus's sacrifice on Calvary was for everyone. The only thing that can prevent anyone from partaking of the promise is his or her choosing not to. The cross is an invitation to all who choose to accept it.

Heavenly Father, we are thankful for the shedding of the blood of Jesus that has made it possible to call on you. I pray my trust in you will be strengthened daily by the power of your Holy Spirit in Jesus's name, amen.

Reflections, Thoughts, and Prayer

_____

_____

_____

_____

_____

_____

_____

_____

February 15

For many are called, but few are chosen.
—Matthew 22:14 (KJV)

"Humility before honor"—a popular quote to remind you that humility is a prerequisite to getting the blessing God has in store for you. To be a servant of the Lord is no small task. It requires you to go where you would never want to go and be in contact with people you would never want to meet. This is probably why few are chosen; how many people are willing to humble themselves and allow God to work through them?

Your life could be one of great success, a life that is full and meaningful, but first, you must remove the pride and surrender all to God.

Heavenly Father, I desire to humble myself before you today. I want to bring glory to you. I want to be sealed with the seal of the Living God. I want to be chosen by you. I pray for your Holy Spirit and ask you to work with me a little longer as I strive to me more like Jesus, amen.

Reflections, Thoughts, and Prayer

February 16

> And Elijah came unto all the people, and said, how
> long halt ye between two opinions? If the LORD be
> God, follow him: but if Baal, then follow him.
> —1 Kings 18:21 (KJV)

*S*in is the transgression of God's law. This is given in the holy scriptures. Those who claim to be followers of God but do whatever they desire show they do not know the Word of the Living God. God is the leader of His children. The map is the Bible. It is important to search the scriptures prayerfully to know the voice of God; He says, "My sheep will follow if they hear my voice." We will know the truth, and as more and more truth is revealed, may we make our choice clear so all will know we are following the Lord.

Heavenly Father, I want my character to show I am a follower of Jesus Christ, my Lord and Savior, amen.

Reflections, Thoughts, and Prayer

_____

_____

_____

_____

_____

_____

_____

February 17

O God, thou art my God; early will I seek thee:
my soul thirsteth for thee, my flesh longeth for thee
in a dry and thirsty land, where no water is.
—Psalm 63:1 (KJV)

The odds against Asa were enormous. There were a million of men in arms against him, besides three hundred chariots. It seemed impossible to hold his own against that vast multitude. There were no allies who would come to his help; his only hope, therefore, was in God. It may be that your difficulties have been allowed to come to so alarming a pitch that you may be compelled to renounce all creature aid, to which in lesser trials you have had recourse, and cast yourself back on your Almighty Friend. (SD 1/5)

*H*eavenly Father, my soul is thirsty for you, and I have a hunger to know more about the life of Jesus. Help me trust you more by the power of your Holy Spirit. That is my prayer in Jesus's name, amen.

Reflections, Thoughts, and Prayer

_____

_____

_____

_____

_____

February 18

The Lord is not slack concerning his promise.
—2 Peter 3:9 (KJV)

God knows the need of His children. He is neither forgetful nor neglectful about what He has promised. While living in this wicked land, the Lord continues to lead and protect His beloved. He allows affliction to come in the way of the righteous so purification can take place and many can witness the unwavering faith and consistent course of those who are called by Christ's name.

Eternal Father, there is no better place to be than in your hands. Trusting that you have only our best interest at heart, build my faith in you, mold me, and fashion me until I become what you would have me be in Jesus's name, amen.

Reflections, Thoughts, and Prayer

_____

_____

_____

_____

_____

_____

_____

February 19

Glory to God in the highest, and on earth
peace, good will toward men.
—Luke 2:14 (KJV)

The peace that passes all understanding is given to all who will accept the teachings of Christ. This is a gospel of peace, love, and harmony. It can unite brother and brother and creation to Creator. To receive this peace, one must receive Jesus. Give Him permission to come into your heart. Give glory to Him who is worthy.

Heavenly Father, we come before you longing for the peace only you can give. We accept the gift Jesus has given us—access to you directly—and we want to live in harmony with our families, neighbors, friends, colleagues, and all those to whom we witness daily with the way we are living our lives. Give us your Holy Spirit I pray, amen.

Reflections, Thoughts, and Prayer

_____

_____

_____

_____

_____

_____

February 20

And be not conformed to this world: but be ye transformed
by the renewing of your mind, that ye may prove what
is that good, and acceptable, and perfect, will of God.
—Romans 12:2 (KJV)

Renew your mind in the Word of God. Make room in your heart for the love of Jesus to reside. When you study His Word and apply it to your life, you will grow day by day more like Christ. Take on His righteousness, and live the life Christ has called you to live, a life conformed to the divine nature of God.

Oh to be like the lovely Jesus is my prayer. Heavenly Father, I pray you will keep me on this straight and narrow path that leads to eternity because I was created for your glory and I desire to glorify your name for Christ's sake, amen.

Reflections, Thoughts, and Prayer

_____

_____

_____

_____

_____

_____

_____

February 21

Hatred stirreth up strifes: but love covereth all sins.
—Proverbs 10:12 (KJV)

*L*ove always wants to see the best in all people. Just as Jesus has covered our sins with His blood, we need to learn to cover the sins of those who are close and dear to us. Learn to go to them in love to show them the error of their ways, and after confronting them, let it end right there. No need to tell it to the world.

Heavenly Father, we thank you for a glimpse of love so profound and unconditional that no human mind can know the full extent of it. But we see it in action in nature and among those who aspire to be more like Jesus. I pray your Holy Spirit will help me humble myself so others may get a glimpse of your love as well, amen.

Reflections, Thoughts, and Prayer

_____

_____

_____

_____

_____

_____

_____

_____

February 22

For thou shalt forget the shame of thy youth.
—Isaiah 54:4 (KJV)

*H*ave faith in God. He is faithful and can be trusted. Whatever your past may hold that causes shame, the all-wise God is able to toss it into the sea of forgetfulness. We have the promise that He hears us even before we utter the words of prayer.

God can give you a new life; there is no sin the blood of His Son cannot cleanse, and there is no soul so far gone that He can't set it free.

Heavenly Father, we have all come with different petitions before your holy throne room today. Some are praying for their families to be restored, some for healing, some for financial breakthroughs, and some to live a life that will bring glory to you. Whatever the petition, we pray you will answer favorably in Jesus's name, amen.

Reflections, Thoughts, and Prayer

_____

_____

_____

_____

_____

_____

February 23

The pride of thine heart hath deceived thee.
—Obadiah 1:3 (KJV)

*L*et us never lose sight of God. We are wholly dependent on Him. When Saul was first called to be king, he trusted in God and looked to Him for instruction on how he should lead. But soon, he became self-confident; he trusted in himself and his success. All humility was gone. He was king. He wanted to be loved and exalted; in his heart, he had no room left for the Savior.

Dear Lord and Father of humanity, forgive our foolish ways. We are a people whom you have chosen to be your special agents, and we have allowed so much of self to come between you and us. We need to learn from you. As we study and learn about the life Jesus lived on earth, we become changed and unashamedly humble ourselves, and we follow His way we pray, amen.

Reflections, Thoughts, and Prayer

February 24

Seek him that maketh the seven stars and Orion,
and turneth the shadow of death into the morning,
and maketh the day dark with night: that calleth for
the waters of the sea, and poureth them out upon
the face of the earth: The LORD is his name.
—Amos 5:8 (KJV)

Take time to look at the heavens. Look at the stars and know whom you serve. God is great!

Heavenly Father, I thank you for reminding us of your majestic power and might. Father, we realize you are God and God alone. Thank you for the beauty of the earth and the loving reminders that we serve a God who has good plans for us, who calls us out of a world of chaos and misery, and sets us up as His special agents to bring the wonderful message of salvation to those who are languishing in darkness. I pray to be a faithful and true representative of Jesus for His name's sake, amen.

Reflections, Thoughts, and Prayer

_____

_____

_____

_____

_____

_____

February 25

O LORD our Lord, how excellent is thy
name in all the earth!
—Psalm 8:9 (KJV)

God wants us to enjoy all He has created for us. He took special care to prepare all things—from the birds in the air to the fish in the sea. Each leaf with its unique print shows us how great God is. All nature was created for our pleasure. After He made all the necessary preparations, He took special care to create us in His image. With a Father's love, He watched Adam and Eve delight in all He had given them. He desires the same for us today. Take time to learn of God through nature. Look at the vast sea, the tall trees of the forest, the tireless spiders, and the litter of kittens. See how great God is!

When we consider all you have created for our enjoyment, all we can do is praise and magnify your name for you are good and your mercy endures forever, amen.

Reflections, Thoughts, and Prayer

_____

_____

_____

_____

_____

February 26

And it shall come to pass, that whosoever shall call
on the name of the LORD shall be delivered.
—Joel 2:32 (KJV)

We are living in an age of doubt. The Christian life is full of faithlessness and unbelief. Even those who claim to be looking for their Lord's return are not all true to their principles. We need to develop a childlike faith that takes God at His word. By His Holy Spirit, we can begin to apply habits to our lives that will trust our Father knowing He has our best interest close to His heart.

My Lord, I am guilty of not believing as I should. I pray your Holy Spirit will help me develop that childlike faith and not waver in it. I ask for a daily conversion in my heart so the Christian life will not be cheapened but will draw others to you for Christ's sake, amen.

Reflections, Thoughts, and Prayer

_____

_____

_____

_____

_____

_____

_____

February 27

> Then was our mouth filled with laughter,
> and our tongue with singing.
> —Psalm 126:2 (KJV)

*L*et us talk more of God and His goodness. He is constantly blessing us, but we take very little time to talk about Him and His love. When we laugh, we should give Him thanks. When we wake up full of life and energy, we should give Him thanks. When we make it home after a treacherous day, we should give Him thanks. If we thought of God as often as we have evidence of His care for us, we would keep Him ever in our thoughts and would delight to tell others about Him.

Heavenly Father, may you be exalted and praised by all, but may my life be one of praise even today I ask in Jesus's name, amen.

Reflections, Thoughts, and Prayer

_____

_____

_____

_____

_____

_____

_____

February 28

When thou goest, thy steps shall not be straitened;
and when thou runnest, thou shalt not stumble.
—Proverbs 4:12 (KJV)

There is not a need to worry about future and unforeseen obstacles. Remember that God is with you ever by your side. As you go through life, remember that when the time is just right, whatever difficulties come, God is there and will show you the way at just the right time. Trust His heart.

Heavenly Father, we depend entirely on you and surrender our hearts to you. We turn from our wicked ways and ask for pardon. May the Holy Spirit help us turn our eyes heavenward and keep them fixed steadfast on Jesus we pray, amen.

Reflections, Thoughts, and Prayer

_____

_____

_____

_____

_____

_____

_____

February 29

And there we saw the giants ... and we were in our own
sight as grasshoppers, and so we were in their sight.
—Numbers 13:33 (KJV)

*T*he Israelites lost sight of the fact God was in their midst. They complained about Moses and accused God of taking them from Egypt into the wilderness and promising them a land that was too difficult to attain. They wished to go back to slavery. Have you lost sight of God?

Thank you, Father, for calling us out of darkness into your marvelous light. Thank you for cleansing us and giving us the honored responsibility of being watchmen on the walls of the beautiful city. We pray we all open our eyes and see how majestic you are. We have no need to fear the giants or circumstances of our lives; we just need to walk trusting you in Jesus's name, amen.

Reflections, Thoughts, and Prayer

_____

_____

_____

_____

_____

_____

March 1

And when Peter was come down out of the ship,
he walked on the water, to go to Jesus. But when
he saw the wind boisterous, he was afraid; and
beginning to sink, he cried, saying, Lord, save me.
—Matthew 14:29–30 (KJV)

Peter was the only one of the twelve disciples who walked on water. Faith mingled with unbelief allowed Peter to lose sight of his Savior for but one moment. In that moment, Peter began to sink, but he knew the power of prayer, a one-phrase prayer, "Lord, save me." Though Jesus was next to Peter, Peter forgot the power of his Redeemer. Pray for increase in faith.

Loving Redeemer, may we never take our eyes off you lest we fall. May we meditate on your life here on earth. When we fix our eyes on you, we can do unbelievable, extraordinary things. Thank you for always being by our side. Help us rise to the occasion by the power of your Holy Spirit we pray, amen.

Reflections, Thoughts, and Prayer

_____

_____

_____

_____

_____

_____

March 2

For your shame ye shall have double.
—Isaiah 61:7 (KJV)

*C*hristians ought to be full of joy and gladness. It is their duty to convince the world that God can give them beauty for their ashes. A mournful, complaining Christian is not a Christian.

Your life should be full of evidence of the presence of Jesus. It is not a life free of trials and disappointments, but the presence of His strength will see you through.

Heavenly Father, I come before you with joy and gladness thanking you for all you have done. I claim the promise I will have double for my shame. No matter what I may be going through, I know it is only for a season and Christ will vindicate me for His name's sake, amen.

Reflections, Thoughts, and Prayer

_____

_____

_____

_____

_____

_____

_____

March 3

A friend loveth at all times, and a brother
is born for adversity.
—Proverbs 17:17 (KJV)

Every association we form, however limited, exerts
some influence upon us. The extent to which we yield
to that influence will be determined by the degree of
intimacy, the constancy of the intercourse, and our love
and veneration for the one with whom we associate.
(SD 166.3)

*M*ost kind and loving Father, I thank you for those you have placed
in my path for such a time as this. They are people I know I can
count on to defend my name and honor in times of adversity. Thank you
for friends who love at all times and want to see good for me and not
evil. And as we call each other brother and sister, may we be deserving
of that name; that is my prayer, amen.

Reflections, Thoughts, and Prayer

_____

_____

_____

_____

_____

_____

March 4

> Arise, be not slothful to go, and to enter to possess
> the land. A place where there is no want
> of any thing that is in the earth.
> —Judges 18:9–10 (KJV)

God is looking for men and women who are willing to hold the fort. There may be obstacles and harsh, bumpy roads ahead, but these few will labor for their Maker without murmuring. Let us ask the Lord for His Spirit so we may be converted and experience the joy of the Lord. He has assured us His yoke is easy. He will never give us more than we can bear, but we must answer His call and be obedient in service.

I pray for an active spirit to be developed in me, so every day I will do what is before me knowing you, O Lord, are guiding my steps in Jesus's name, amen.

Reflections, Thoughts, and Prayer

_____

_____

_____

_____

_____

_____

March 5

Rejoice in the Lord alway: and again I say, rejoice.
—Philippians 4:4 (KJV)

*L*et us practice speaking words of wisdom and kindness one to another. As we are preparing for heaven, where we will live one in Christ, our words and works need to show we are like the Lamb of heaven. Let us praise God in all we do and give thanks to Him who has cleansed us from all unrighteousness.

Heavenly Father, I pray for a right spirit in me. Please remove all bitterness, anger, jealousy, hatred, and unkind words from me and replace that with your joy, peace, trust, and love. I pray in Jesus's name, amen.

Reflections, Thoughts, and Prayer

_____

_____

_____

_____

_____

_____

_____

_____

March 6

The joy of the LORD is your strength.
—Nehemiah 8:10 (KJV)

A Christian's life is full of joy and thanksgiving. Though it is not free from trial, it should not be marked with gloom. We should live a life that God can bless, a life that will bring Him much honor. Our heavenly Father does not want us in darkness and self-depreciation. Walking with our heads bowed is not a sign of true humility. Get on your knees and talk to your Creator, and mercy and cleansing of sin will take place. We are able to walk with heads lifted because of the sacrifice of Christ. Let us honor Him.

Loving Redeemer, I am grateful for your sacrificing yourself so I can face tomorrow with hope, gladness, and great expectations. I want to be blessed by you, and I want to reach the full potential a sinner like me can reach for your name's sake, amen.

Reflections, Thoughts, and Prayer

_____

_____

_____

_____

_____

_____

To him will I give the land that he hath trodden upon, and
to his children, because he hath
wholly followed the LORD.
—Deuteronomy 1:36 (KJV)

We here read the warnings, which God gave to ancient Israel. It was not his good pleasure that they should wander so long in the wilderness, and he would have brought them immediately to the promised land, if they had submitted, and loved to be led by him; and because they so often grieved him in the desert, he sware in his wrath that they should not enter into his rest, save two, who wholly followed him. God required his people to trust in him alone. (4bSG 72.1)

Heavenly Father, I stand before you guilty because I know I complain and murmur against you when things are not going my way. Please forgive me and work with me to unlearn the bad habits I've acquired and learn the way you are leading. I pray in Jesus's name, amen.

Reflections, Thoughts, and Prayers

_____

_____

_____

_____

_____

March 8

Is not this the word that we did tell thee in Egypt,
saying, Let us alone, that we may serve the Egyptians?
For it had been better for us to serve the Egyptians,
than that we should die in the wilderness.
—Exodus 14:12 (KJV)

*A*re you being tested today? Life is a series of obstacles that must be tackled one after the other. But the Giver of Life allows these obstacles in your way to see just how much you trust His leading. Praise the Lord in the good as well as the bad times. Pass the test.

Heavenly Father, you have taken me out of Egypt to a land flowing with milk and honey. I pray you will take Egypt out of me because of the complaining, gossiping, and murmuring that exist in me. Forgive me, and give me the victory to trust you in Jesus's name I pray, amen.

Reflections, Thoughts, and Prayer

March 9

Iron sharpeneth iron; so a man sharpeneth
the countenance of his friend.
—Proverbs 27:17 (KJV)

The Exodus serves as an example of what not to do when the presence of God is leading. With every difficulty that presented itself, the people forgot the miracle that was done before, they forgot God was in their midst. Instead of praising God, the complained; instead of thanking God, they demanded more with an ungrateful attitude saying, "Would God that we had died when our brethren died before the Lord" (Numbers 20:3 KJV).

Heavenly Father, I'm thankful for those you have placed in my life to inspire me, encourage me, and elevate me to newer heights. Help me to sharpen my skills in you so I may be an influence of good to those I encounter. May I look to you in prayer when choosing my friends I pray in Jesus's name, amen.

Reflections, Thoughts, and Prayer

_____

_____

_____

_____

_____

_____

March 10

> For Christ sent me not to baptize, but to preach
> the gospel: not with wisdom of words, lest the
> cross of Christ should be made of none effect.
> —1 Corinthians 1:17 (KJV)

Throughout the ages, humanity has devised plans on how to serve God. The Bible says everyone did what seemed good in his or her eyes. If the world says it is good, the majority of people say it is good even when it contradicts the Word of the Living God. God is compassionate and long-suffering, but people take that for granted.

There is a limit to sin. It is now that you need to choose to be on God's side. There's our plan, and then there's God's plan. God's plan is always best.

Heavenly Father, forgive us for thinking our way is best when it leads us to destruction over and over. I desire to know you, and I desire to live a life that speaks of you by the power of your Holy Spirit, amen.

Reflections, Thoughts, and Prayer

_____

_____

_____

_____

_____

_____

March 11

Then said Jesus, Father, forgive them;
for they know not what they do.
—Luke 23:34 (KJV)

The pain and agony that crushed our Redeemer was more than you and I could ever imagine. Rejected by those He came to save, spat on, beaten, and mocked, He nonetheless took on and the sins of everyone once and for all. Oh how He suffered. Through all the suffering, the feeling of separation from His Father pierced Him the most. He cried out, "My God, my God, why hast thou forsaken me?" Let's learn from our loving Savior. When we fail to feel the presence of God, we should know God is very near encouraging us to go forward.

Dear Jesus, I'm sorry every time I sin; I know it causes you pain. I pray for your Holy Spirit to breathe on me so I may have the victory once and for all. I thank you for thinking of me on Calvary. My desire is to make you proud for your name's sake, amen.

Reflections, Thoughts, and Prayers

_____

_____

_____

_____

_____

March 12

Yet I am not alone, because the Father is with me.
—John 16:32 (KJV)

*W*hen Christ walked among us, He sought to alleviate the pain and suffering of those around Him. Now, He intercedes in heaven on our behalf. His tender, loving heart has not changed. He desires all those who are called by His name be free from sin.

When you pray, believe and it will be so.

Loving Savior, it's good to know you are always with us and can empathize and sympathize with all our temptations. You yourself were tempted on all points but did not sin. I give thanks for your blood that pardons and gives me strength from moment to moment knowing it will never lose its power! Hallelujah!

Reflections, Thoughts, and Prayer

March 13

> For we have not an high priest which cannot be
> touched with the feeling of our infirmities; but was in
> all points tempted like as we are, yet without sin.
> —Hebrews 4:15 (KJV)

What a wonderful thing it is to serve a risen Savior who is acquainted with all our trials. He was tempted on all points but sinned not. He overcame, and by His Holy Spirit, we too are more than conquerors. He does not leave us to struggle alone with sin; we have the Comforter and the angels to show us how we too might overcome.

Heavenly Father, we thank you for making a way to draw all humanity to you through Jesus Christ, your Son. I pray for the blood of Jesus to sanctify and restore all who are willing to be cleansed. I ask your Holy Spirit to live in my heart in Jesus's name, amen.

Reflections, Thoughts, and Prayer

_____

_____

_____

_____

_____

_____

_____

_____

March 14

> And the people thirsted there for water; and the
> people murmured against Moses, and said, Wherefore
> is this that thou hast brought us up out of Egypt, to
> kill us and our children and our cattle with thirst?
> —Exodus 17:3 (KJV)

Followers of God must separate themselves from the world: "The friendship of the world is enmity with God; whosoever therefore will be a friend of the world is the enemy of God" (James 4:4). We are a distinct and peculiar people, and that difference needs to be clear. We must choose whom we associate with carefully lest we be led down the wrong path.

Heavenly Father, help us look to the past to see the way in which you have led us so when the difficulties of life present themselves, we will be firmly grounded on a "Thus said the Lord," amen.

Reflections, Thoughts, and Prayer

_____

_____

_____

_____

_____

_____

March 15

He that walketh with wise men shall be wise:
but a companion of fools shall be destroyed.
—Proverbs 13:20 (KJV)

Choose your friends carefully. If you are the wisest among your friends, it's time to add new friends to your circle. Pray and ask God to open doors for you to meet people who will help you reach your full potential. Being complacent and mundane does not depict a true reflection of Christ. Look around you; there are so many interesting things, so many venues to explore, species to discover, and people to meet. In the process, let the Holy Spirit work in you so you can be one of the wise whom others seek to know.

Heavenly Father, I ask you to help me to choose my friends carefully. I ask you to put me in the company of wise people so I may reflect your beauty and sweet fragrance of kindness and wisdom to others all around by the power of your Holy Spirit. I know I can, amen.

Reflections, Thoughts, and Prayer

_____

_____

_____

_____

_____

_____

I drew them with cords of a man, with bands of love.
—Hosea 11:4 (KJV)

*O*ur caring and loving attitude must be so attractive that all we encounter will be blessed and refreshed after spending some time with us. That is what it means to be a Christian. You have the privilege to influence others for the better and touch lives in a way that will enhance and not destroy. When you think you have nothing to give, remember to smile and show others the kindness God has shown you.

My heavenly Father, I need you because without you I can do nothing. Like Paul, I want to do good, but I find myself doing wrong. I ask that if you are able to use a vessel like me, please use me for I am willing but the flesh is weak. Empower me by your Holy Spirit I pray in Jesus's name, amen.

Reflections, Thoughts, and Prayer

_____

_____

_____

_____

_____

_____

March 17

I die daily.
—1 Corinthians 15:31 (KJV)

To die daily takes real effort; it requires denying the self. It is not enough to deny self; we must sacrifice self. Make yourself available to serve. Take time to visit the sick, give comfort to the hurting, show kindness to the outcasts, be patient with the unlearned, fortify the weak with the Word of the Living God, and make time for the children and the elderly. Remember that by their fruit you will know who are Christians.

Heavenly Father, in Jesus I die daily to self and trust the leading of your Holy Spirit. I pray for victory over all my thoughts, words, and action. I pray for self-control and to develop the fruit of the Spirit today in Jesus's name, amen.

Reflections, Thoughts, and Prayer

_____

_____

_____

_____

_____

_____

March 18

Wherefore, my beloved, as ye have always obeyed, not as
in my presence only, but now much more in my absence,
work out your own salvation with fear and trembling.
—Philippians 2:12 (KJV)

True success in any line of work is not the result of
chance or accident or destiny. It is the outworking of
God's providences, the reward of faith and discretion,
of virtue and perseverance. Fine mental qualities and
a high moral tone are not the result of accident. God
gives opportunities; success depends upon the use made
of them. (CSA 56.1)

*H*eavenly Father, we need spiritual eyes so we can see and seize the
opportunities when they come. We pray for spiritual understanding
of your precious and holy Word so we might understand the time in
which we are living. And as we understand, may we look to you to guide
our steps. We pray this in Jesus's name, amen.

Reflections, Thoughts, and Prayer

_____

_____

_____

_____

_____

March 19

Be not deceived: evil communications
corrupt good manners.
—1 Corinthians (KJV)

*T*hose who claim to be children of God should display evidence of uprightness in their everyday talk, integrity in the workplace, devotion to God, and their representation of Christ in a well-ordered, godly life.

All you do should glorify God. Everyone you encounter should feel the same love, mercy, and respect from you as given to you by your heavenly Father because every soul is precious to Him. Saints and sinners alike are precious in His sight and deserve the same treatment as has been shown to you. Remember that Christ died so all could live.

Heavenly Father, search my heart and fashion it to love what you love and hate what you hate. I pray for good manners. I don't want to be a stumbling block to someone else. Help me to love as you love. Keep me far from gossip; may I lift you up always I pray, amen.

Reflections, Thoughts, and Prayer

_____

_____

_____

_____

_____

March 20

Looking unto Jesus the author and
finisher of our faith.
—Hebrews 12:2 (KJV)

With every new experience, we should look to Jesus, who desires to be a part of our everyday experiences. Make a habit of talking with Him. He will give you strength to meet every new experience. Whatever life may bring, you will be able to face it with Jesus.

Heavenly Father, we pray for an increase of faith these last days. Our eyes are fixed on you, King Jesus. We look to you to guide our every step along this narrow path. We pray we will be ambassadors representing you as you deserve, but we can do that only by your Holy Spirit. We ask for a double portion even now in Jesus's name, amen.

Reflections, Thoughts, and Prayer

_____

_____

_____

_____

_____

_____

March 21

Now thanks be unto God, which always
causeth us to triumph in Christ.
—2 Corinthians 2:14 (KJV)

*P*aul's life is one worth noting. He didn't have it easy once he decided to spread the gospel. He met with danger at every turn; he encountered hardship he had never expected. His life was threatened time and again. But he trusted in the power of God to deliver him. Paul knew his life was in the life of His Creator. No matter what happened, Paul knew Jesus was in heaven at the right of His Father. So it ought to be with us.

We give thanks to you, Father, who always causes us to triumph in Christ. We know there is stormy weather up ahead these last days, but as Paul and Barnabas did, may we learn to trust in your power to deliver us. We pray this in Jesus's name, amen.

Reflections, Thoughts, and Prayer

_____

_____

_____

_____

_____

_____

March 22

And beside this, giving all diligence, add to
your faith virtue; and to virtue knowledge.
—2 Peter 1:5 (KJV)

Jesus left such an awesome example for all those who chose to follow Him to live in this world but not be a part of it. He didn't partake in all the pleasures and traditions of humanity, but daily, He sought to do His Father's will. He looked for those who had been held captive by sin for so long, those whose hopes were gone. He looked for those who knew they needed a Savior.

Those who choose to follow in His footsteps may stand uncontaminated in whatever surroundings they may find themselves in this world.

Heavenly Father, we desire an increase of faith to witness and lift up *the* man, Christ Jesus. We pray to uphold your standards in a world filled with darkness and traditions of humanity. Help us perform our duty as faithful stewards where you have placed us; that is our prayer in Jesus's name, amen.

Reflections, Thoughts, and Prayer

_____

_____

_____

_____

_____

March 23

For my yoke is easy, and my burden is light.
—Matthew 11:30 (KJV)

God doesn't give trials to His children, but He does permit them. He knows just what they can handle and will be there to help them overcome. God will not forsake you. When the dark clouds begin to set around you, that's the time to pray and activate your faith. He is faithful!

Heavenly Father, we are thankful for our elder brother, Jesus, who knows and understands our trials and difficulties. Today, we bring you all our hardships knowing you have the power to remove the sting this life can bring. We ask you to replace them with your joy and peace, amen.

Reflections, Thoughts, and Prayer

March 24

The tongue of the wise is health.
—Proverbs 12:18 (KJV)

*M*y dear brothers and sisters, how are you using the gift of speech? Have you learned to control your tongue so when you speak wisdom, hope, and comfort, you will revive the weakest of souls? Is your speech free from evil surmising, pride, and backbiting?

Words have a powerful effect on others. They can lift them up or bring them down. Though no one can control the unruly member, we all can look to Christ to help gain the victory moment by moment, day by day.

Heavenly Father, we ask you to take control of our tongues. Season our speech with all that is like you so when we speak, others may be comforted. May your word of love be on our lips in everything we say. We pray this in Jesus's name, amen.

Reflections, Thoughts, and Prayer

_____

_____

_____

_____

_____

_____

March 25

> Blessed are they that mourn:
> for they shall be comforted.
> —Matthew 5:4 (KJV)

Jesus knows how it feels to be lonely. He understands pain, struggles, and temptations. He sees every tear you cry because while here on earth Jesus wept too.

Jesus did not experience anything you haven't experienced. He invites you to come boldly to the throne of grace to find the remedy for your pain.

Heavenly Father, we are thankful that Jesus was tempted in all points as we are but sinned not. It's reassuring to know He knows what we're going through. I pray that an intervention will take place in our lives so the desires in our hearts will come to pass even in these last days of earth's history. We pray this in Jesus's name, amen.

Reflections, Thoughts, and Prayer

_____

_____

_____

_____

_____

_____

March 26

He must increase, but I must decrease.
—John 3:30 (KJV)

*A*s children in Christ, we must grow in knowledge and in the beauty of the loveliness of God. Jesus's character should reveal itself to those with whom we come in contact daily. A deeper walk with God is essential to know God's will for us.

Let your light shine so all may see you are a child of the Living God. If you choose to hide your light under a bushel, you are destroying yourself. And as your faith gets weaker and weaker, you can possibly destroy some around you. That is why Jesus must increase in you every day and your sense of self must decrease.

Heavenly Father, we pray we will learn your ways, not the ways of humanity. We ask for your Holy Spirit to guide us always, and we ask you to help us be stewards of our time so we might devote more time and energy with you. That is our prayer, amen.

Reflections, Thoughts, and Prayers

_____

_____

_____

_____

_____

March 27

And the LORD said unto Samuel ... they
have not rejected thee, but they have rejected
me, that I should not reign over them.
—1 Samuel 8:7 (KJV)

Had Israel been true to her trust, all the nations of
earth would have shared in her blessings. But the hearts
of those to whom had been entrusted a knowledge of
saving truth, were untouched by the needs of those
around them. As God's purpose was lost sight of, the
light of truth was withheld, and darkness prevailed.
The nations were overspread with a veil of ignorance;
the love of God was little known; error and superstition
flourished. (PK 371.1)

*H*eavenly Father, I feel the indifference in my own cold and stony
heart. I pray your Holy Spirit will soften my heart so I may develop
a genuine love for those you came to die for. I pray in Jesus's name,
amen.

Reflections, Thoughts, and Prayer

_____

_____

_____

_____

_____

March 28

Husbands, love your wives, even as Christ also
loved the church, and gave himself for it.
—Ephesians 5:25 (KJV)

*L*ove begins at home. Men, you are the husbands, and your duty as a husband is to love your wife even as Christ also loved the church and was willing to die for her. So it ought to be with the husband; you have to find the one you will protect to the point of death if it should come to that. Don't be impatient with your wife; stop finding faults with every little thing. Instead, show her tenderness, patience, love. How can you lead the church when your home doesn't mimic what's been required by your Creator?

Heavenly Father, today, we pray for our men—fathers, brothers, and sons. You have given them a special role to play, but so few are willing or able to carry out their duty. I pray your Holy Spirit will empower them to be the men you've called them to be in Jesus's name, amen.

Reflections, Thoughts, and Prayer

_____

_____

_____

_____

_____

March 29

> He giveth power to the faint; and to them that
> have no might he increaseth strength.
> —Isaiah 40:29 (KJV)

*Y*es, Satan is powerful, but with all the power he has, he is unable to shake the faith of one who has decided to trust in God. Simple, childlike faith is what God is looking for. God wants you to be wholly dependent on Him. He wants you to abide in Him. He sent His only begotten Son to die for sinners like you and me. He wants to restore broken hearts, dreams, health, and financial situations. Cast all your cares upon Him because He cares for you.

Loving Father, we come to you for an increase in power and strength. These last days can weaken our faith, but we give thanks for your Holy Comforter, who continues to keep us and empower us from day to day. We have a need for Jesus. Please forgive us and heal us we pray for Christ's sake, amen.

Reflections, Thoughts, and Prayer

_____

_____

_____

_____

_____

March 30

Consider the lilies of the field, how they grow.
—Matthew 6:28 (KJV)

Why worry? Worry shows we do not trust God. Look around in nature. Everything is as it should be. The animals seek food and find it. The trees are tall and green; they worry not about the lack of water or too much sun. Everything blooms when it should and grows as it should. If the Lord is able to keep all nature moving in perfect order, how much more is He working in your life? Trust His heart!

At the beginning of this spring season, may we take time to learn from nature knowing that you, heavenly Father, know what we need. Take away our cares and disappointments and fill us with your love in Jesus's name, amen.

Reflections, Thoughts, and Prayer

_____

_____

_____

_____

_____

_____

_____

March 31

And the apostles said unto the Lord,
Increase our faith.
—Luke 17:5 (KJV)

Fellow Christians, you believe in God, and you believe on Him, but have you advanced far enough in your Christian walk to believe Him, that is to believe what He says and all says? Has it ever struck you that we trust the word of our fellow man more easily than we trust God's word? (KC 47)

*A*s the apostles of old did, we pray you will increase our faith. Lord, we are seeing every uncouth thing taking place, and our hearts grow weary and weak. But we continue to look up because we know Jesus's return is closer than it's ever been. We need a childlike faith that will believe in our heavenly Father nothing wavering; we pray this in Jesus's name, amen.

Reflections, Thoughts, and Prayer

_____

_____

_____

_____

_____

_____

April 1

Be patient therefore, brethren, unto the coming of the
Lord. Behold, the husbandman waiteth for the precious
fruit of the earth, and hath long patience for it, until he
receive the early and latter rain. Be ye also patient; stablish
your hearts: for the coming of the Lord draweth nigh.
—James 5:7–8 (KJV)

The time is fast approaching when all we have endured will seem a cheap price to have paid to be in the presence of our Redeemer. He is coming again real soon. Strengthen your faith.

How we long for that day when all trials and sufferings will be as nothingness. We pray we will have the necessary patience to run our race, staying in the faith praising your holy name. We ask for an anointing to take place sealing our children for eternity is our prayer in Jesus's name, amen.

Reflections, Thoughts, and Prayer

_____

_____

_____

_____

_____

_____

April 2

Cast not away therefore your confidence, which hath
great recompence of reward. For ye have need of
patience, that, after ye have done the will of God, ye
might receive the promise. For yet a little while, and
he that shall come will come, and will not tarry.
—Hebrews 10:35–37 (KJV)

How beautiful it is to know Jesus is preparing a place for you and me and will soon return to take us home to the New Jerusalem. Where He is, we will be also. No more pain, no more tears, no more suffering. We will be praising the great I Am because His mercy endures forever.

Heavenly Father, our confidence is in you. I pray for the coming of our Lord and Savior to hasten and for this world of sin and misery to be as it was first created full of beauty and without sin. I look forward to the day when we will be going home, never to part, amen.

Reflections, Thoughts, and Prayer

_____

_____

_____

_____

_____

_____

April 3

But I have prayed for thee, that thy faith fail not: and
when thou art converted, strengthen thy brethren.
—Luke 22:32 (KJV)

*M*issionary John Hyde was being prayed for by a friend to be set free
from the sin that beset him. When it came time for him to preach,
he said, "I could not stand up to preach the gospel until I could testify
of its power in my life." Hyde got the victory due to his praying friend.

Heavenly Father, we desire to know you. We pray for a life where
we pray, study, and claim your promises. We want to constantly look to
you for guidance, and we want to persevere in prayer like Jacob wrestled
with you. Father, we ask for your blessings so we can stand these last
days; we pray this in Jesus's name, amen.

Reflections, Thoughts, and Prayer

_____

_____

_____

_____

_____

_____

_____

April 4

That men may know that thou, whose name alone is
JEHOVAH, art the most high over all the earth.
—Psalm 83:18 (KJV)

Jesus came to this sinful world and was crucified so
that you can ask in His name. Today He I sits on the
throne and He holds to us His scepter of power; prayer.
He yearns to grant us "according to the riches of His
glory." He tells us that our strength and our fruitfulness
depend upon our prayers. He reminds us that our very
joy depends upon answered prayer (John 16:24). (KC 22)

Jehovah, we praise your name for you are worthy! Recognizing that
nothing is left to chance and knowing you sit on the throne that
governs this universe and beyond, we commit our lives into your hand
today in Jesus's name, amen.

Reflections, Thoughts, and Prayer

_____

_____

_____

_____

_____

_____

April 5

Therefore whatsoever ye have spoken in
darkness shall be heard in the light.
—Luke 12:3 (KJV)

Whatever good you are doing for the Master, let it be Him who speaks of your good works. Those who make the mistake of exalting themselves are only deceiving their own souls. A healthy person who follows the laws of health does not go around saying he is healthy; he allows his life to speak of his health. He is present at the job and lives to a ripe old age, and the joy and vitality of life is worth noticing. So it is with a person who is living a righteous life. There's no need to constantly tell someone of all the righteous things being done. Let the record speak for itself.

Heavenly Father, I desire to live a life that honors and reflects you. That my public as well as private life makes you proud I pray in Jesus's mighty name, amen.

Reflections, Thoughts, and Prayer

_____

_____

_____

_____

_____

_____

April 6

That the trial of your faith, being much more
precious than of gold that perisheth, though it be
tried with fire, might be found unto praise and
honour and glory at the appearing of Jesus Christ.
—1 Peter 1:7 (KJV)

I asked the angel why there was no more faith and
power in Israel. He said, "Ye let go of the arm of the
Lord too soon. Press your petitions to the throne, and
hold on by strong faith. The promises are sure." (EW
73.2)

*H*eavenly Father, we continue to press our petitions before you in
prayer and exercise the measure of faith given to us. We pray for
healing physically, emotionally, mentally, and spiritually. We pray for
financial doors to open, and we pray for unity among our families.
We ask to remain prisoners of hope believing in your promises, and
we await the day when every promise will be a reality; we pray this in
Jesus's name, amen.

Reflections, Thoughts, and Prayer

_____

_____

_____

_____

_____

_____

April 7

Be sober, be vigilant; because your adversary the devil, as a
roaring lion, walketh about, seeking whom he may devour.
—1 Peter 5:8–9 (KJV)

The enemy of souls is making it his business to study your every move. He is at the workplace, at the playground, and at the home watching your every move to catch you off guard so he can sow his evil seed wherever it may take root. It is in your best interest to make Jesus your guide. Pray for Christ's guidance daily. Ask Him to direct your path. Pray for His Spirit to descend afresh. Ask for a new dose of His Spirit so you can win every battle against self. The enemy knows he has but a short time. If there was ever a time to pray, it is now.

Heavenly Father, we lift up our schools, teachers, and students worldwide. It's evident we have strayed from the original blueprint, and for that we ask your forgiveness. We pray your holy angels will protect our children from influences that have crept into our homes and schools unawares. Help us to magnify your name we pray, amen.

Reflections, Thoughts, and Prayers

April 8

Therefore to him that knoweth to do good,
and doeth it not, to him it is sin.
—James 4:17 (KJV)

Indifference and neutrality have no place in a Christian's heart. If you are in a position to do good, do it when the moment calls for it. Every soul is precious to our Father. All we have been given is to help others come to know our Father's love.

Heavenly Father, you have done so much for us and have given all you have to set us free from sin and redeem us to you. For this, we thank you. We pray and ask you to open our spiritual eyes so we might see those who are in need and reach out and help. May we be wise like serpents but gentle as doves; we pray this in Jesus's name, amen.

Reflections, Thoughts, and Prayer

_____

_____

_____

_____

_____

_____

_____

April 9

Now unto him that is able to keep you from
falling, and to present you faultless before the
presence of his glory with exceeding joy.
—Jude 1:24 (KJV)

*D*o not forget that God is with you in your time of darkest pain. He reminds you that even in the valley of the shadow of death, He is by your side. Call on Him and He will answer. No need to carry such a heavy load on your shoulders. Give it to the one who has paid the price on the cross at Calvary. Give all your burdens to Jesus. Leave them at His feet. Allow His Holy Spirit to break through the shadows and lift your heart to the Son.

Loving Father, we do need to trust you more on the mountaintop as well as in the valley. We pray we will cast all our cares on you because we know in whom we believe. Empower us with your Holy Spirit we pray in Jesus's name, amen.

Reflections, Thoughts, and Prayer

April 10

Here is the patience of the saints: here are they that keep
the commandments of God, and the faith of Jesus.
—Revelation 14:12 (KJV)

It is no easy thing to be a follower of Jesus Christ. Look at what happened to most of Christ's disciples; they died gruesome deaths. Study what took place during the Reformation and you will conclude it is no easy task to be a follower of God. However, Jesus Himself is constantly lifting those who have made up their minds to embrace this gospel of peace up to our Father. He continues to intercede on our behalf guiding our minds to the most holy place always.

We pray for an increase of faith, loving Father, to develop patience as await the second coming of Jesus. We pray to be able to stand up for truth and keep your Commandments though the heavens should fall. We pray for your Holy Spirit in Jesus's name, amen.

Reflections, Thoughts, and Prayer

_____

_____

_____

_____

_____

_____

_____

April 11

> Beloved, when I gave all diligence to write unto you of
> the common salvation, it was needful for me to write unto
> you, and exhort you that ye should earnestly contend for
> the faith which was once delivered unto the saints. For
> there are certain men crept in unawares, who were before
> of old ordained to this condemnation, ungodly men,
> turning the grace of our God into lasciviousness, and
> denying the only Lord God, and our Lord Jesus Christ.
> —Jude 1:3–4 (KJV)

Is there anything on earth worth losing heaven for? If we lose heaven, we lose everything! Let us ask His Holy Spirit to remove, replace, and correct whatever defects that would keep us out of the New Jerusalem so we can reflect the splendid image of Christ.

Heavenly Father, help us contend for the faith that was once delivered unto the saints. It is our desire to make it into heaven. We need the aid of your Holy Spirit to mold us to be more like Jesus, amen.

Reflections, Thoughts, and Prayer

_____

_____

_____

_____

_____

April 12

But the path of the just is as the shining light, that
shineth more and more unto the perfect day.
—Proverbs 4:18 (KJV)

As we get close to God, we will begin to radiate His glory. Remember that when Moses came down from Mount Sinai with the Ten Commandments, which God wrote with His own hands, he was shining. He looked like someone who has been with the great I Am. So it ought to be with every one of us who has chosen to accept the invitation to follow Christ. Let your light shine.

We are thankful for the experiences that have strengthened our faith knowing you are guiding our steps by the power of your Holy Spirit. We pray we will choose to follow you daily until your second return to take us home so we might be where you are always, amen.

Reflections, Thoughts, and Prayer

_____

_____

_____

_____

_____

_____

_____

April 13

For the love of money is the root of all evil.
—1 Timothy 6:10 (KJV)

God has blessed us with health and opportunities to acquire and make money. For this, we give thanks. But when we begin to love the gift more than the Giver, it becomes an issue. The Bible does not condemn the rich because they are rich; being rich is not a sin. But when you will do just about anything to acquire that wealth including cheating, lying, or stealing, you need to come to God and repent. God wants you to use the talents He has given to be blessed and be a blessing to others.

Heavenly Father, we give you thanks for the opportunity you have given us to sustain ourselves, our loved ones, and those in need. We ask that we will help to advance your cause so every kindred, tongue, and nation will know Jesus Christ is alive, amen.

Reflections, Thoughts, and Prayer

_____

_____

_____

_____

_____

_____

_____

April 14

It is better to dwell in a corner of the housetop,
than with a brawling woman in a wide house.
—Proverbs 21:9 (KJV)

The character you have now will be the same character you will have upon Christ's return unless you allow the Holy Spirit to mold you and clean out your heart. The Christian home should be one of joy, peace, and all that is lovely. Father, mother, and children must worship together as well as individually seeking the guidance and wisdom of God. The parents are responsible for the atmosphere of the home. So be at peace one with another.

Heavenly Father, we need your Holy Spirit to overcome self. We pray for a sweet fragrance in our homes. We pray for all mothers, fathers, and children. We ask that you convert them anew as they prepare here on earth for Christ's soon return, amen.

Reflections, Thoughts, and Prayer

_____

_____

_____

_____

_____

_____

April 15

The proverbs of Solomon. A wise son maketh a glad
father: but a foolish son is the heaviness of his mother.
—Proverbs 10:1 (KJV)

Those who have been blessed by the Lord with a child have been
given a grave responsibility to mold and fashion this young mind
and develop the character to that of Christ. Please do not waste precious
resources on spoiling your child; put all your energy into improving your
child's character. Upon Jesus's return, He will come to take those who
are ready. Jesus does not change the character when He comes back.
The preparation time is now.

Heavenly Father, today, we are lifting up the homes to you. We
pray for every family member. We pray for husbands to love their
wives and for wives to submit to their husbands. We pray for a loving,
respectful atmosphere so children can see the beauty of a Christian
home. Strengthen your children we pray in Jesus's name, amen.

Reflections, Thoughts, and Prayer

_____

_____

_____

_____

_____

_____

April 16

But he that refraineth his lips is wise.
—Proverbs 10:19 (KJV)

*A*s Christians, we have the duty to pray, control our thoughts, and prevent negative emotions from creeping into our hearts. The enemy seeks to take away our joy. He is pleased when we wallow in self-pity and murmur against God. We must counteract the power of darkness.

Praise God when you feel the melancholy feelings setting in. Recite a psalm, sing a song, and take a firm hold on your tongue so you will not say something against God that you will regret.

Heavenly Father, we who are called by your name are asking for help in learning to keep our peace. We pray that as we learn to depend wholly on you just as a child depends on his father, we will once again have the joy and peace we once knew as children, amen.

Reflections, Thoughts, and Prayer

_____

_____

_____

_____

_____

_____

_____

April 17

Do all things without murmurings and disputings.
—Philippians 2:14 (KJV)

We are to pray one for another and with each other to lift up the dark clouds that seek to destroy our joy. A joyful and active spirit is very attractive when we are seeking the lost.

If you are constantly grouchy, irritated, and frowning, work on yourself because you might do more harm than good in seeking lost souls. Being happy is a choice. Choose to meditate on all the things that are good, pure, and holy. You can ponder on the Word of God. You can think of His many blessings. Do not let the slightest thing throw you off track. Remember that God is with you. He will help you with any effort you make to change your attitude. Have faith in Him.

Heavenly Father, we pray for a true conversion to take place among us. Help us rejoice and give thanks no matter what the circumstances. We can do it only with your Holy Spirit, amen.

Reflections, Thoughts, and Prayer

_____

_____

_____

_____

_____

April 18

That at the name of Jesus every knee should bow, of
things in heaven, and things in earth, and things under
the earth; And that every tongue should confess that
Jesus Christ is Lord, to the glory of God the Father.
—Philippians 2:10–11 (KJV)

What a merciful and long-suffering God we serve. His love knows no bounds. His mercy endures forever. When we think how for six thousand–plus years the controversy between good and evil has been going on, we realize He is patient with humanity. The day is fast approaching when those who are against Jesus will bow and declare He is God and worthy to be praised.

Heavenly Father, we long for that day when all injustice will be done away with. But we know you are fighting for us and are on our side. We pray you will deliver us from injustice today as we await Christ's soon coming, amen.

Reflections, Thoughts, and Prayer

_____

_____

_____

_____

_____

_____

April 19

He hath sent me to heal the brokenhearted, to preach
deliverance to the captives, and recovering of sight to
the blind, to set at liberty them that are bruised.
—Luke 4:18 (KJV)

Christ came to save humanity. He is acquainted with sorrow and grief. It would do us good to meditate daily on his life and behold His beauty. When we contemplate His holiness, we begin to see our defects and weaknesses as they really are. We will see in what state we truly are living in—imprisoned in sin. Jesus came to set us free and to live in harmony with heaven. By His Spirit, we can.

Thank you, heavenly Father, for your infinite mercy and grace. We are broken and are held captive by our sins. We daily surrender our carnal nature to you and pray you would have thine own way, Lord, for you are the Potter and we are the clay. Restore your image in us we ask in Jesus's name.

Reflections, Thoughts, and Prayer

_____

_____

_____

_____

_____

_____

_____

April 20

Blessing, and honour, and glory, and power,
be unto him that sitteth upon the throne,
and unto the Lamb for ever and ever.
—Revelation 5:13 (KJV)

Beware of Flattery—I am pained when I see men praised, flattered, and petted. God has revealed to me the fact that some who receive these attentions are unworthy to take His name upon their lips; yet they are exalted to heaven in the estimation of finite beings, who read only from outward appearance ... never pet and flatter poor, fallible, erring men, either young or old, married or unmarried. You know not their weaknesses, and you know not but that these very attentions and this profuse praise may prove their ruin. (AH 335.1)

Heavenly Father, we pray our minds will remain on you and the sacrifice of your only begotten Son, Jesus, who has made it possible to have access to your holy throne room. He is the one worthy of all our praises, amen.

Reflections, Thoughts, and Prayer

_____

_____

_____

_____

_____

April 21

For God so loved the world, that he gave his only
begotten Son, that whosoever believeth in him
should not perish, but have everlasting life.
—John 3:16 (KJV)

God's gifts to His children are new and fresh every day. When you look at all the varieties there are in nature, you can appreciate that He is ever so creative and full of abundance. So it is with His gifts to us. The greatest gift still remains the gift of His only begotten Son, who willingly came to die for all humanity.

Heavenly Father, thank you for the most wonderful gift of all, the gift of your beloved Son, Jesus. Today, we are free from the sins of the world because of His blood. We pray we will live lives that reflect your love for us so all the world may see we are blessed, amen.

Reflections, Thoughts, and Prayer

_____

_____

_____

_____

_____

_____

_____

April 22

For the great day of his wrath is come;
and who shall be able to stand?
—Revelation 6:17 (KJV)

When an opportunity presents itself for improving your character and life, you should take total advantage in following through with it. Those who fail to seize moments like these will soon find that their character is not reflecting Christ.

You must build your faith and grow in Christ so when trial and temptation come your way, you'll be able to stand. Too often, you are discouraged under stressful situations. Your faith vanishes under persecution because the foundation is not solid. I implore you to look up to Jesus. He is the Rock on which your kingdom needs to be build. Look to Jesus and you will be able to stand.

Heavenly Father, we ask for forgiveness because we murmur when the trials come instead of singing your praises because we fail to realize you are preparing us for the day when we will have to stand without a Mediator. May we learn to trust you we pray, amen.

Reflections, Thoughts, and Prayer

April 23

And the men of Beth-shemesh said, Who is
able to stand before this holy LORD God?
—1 Samuel 6:20 (KJV)

*W*ho shall be able to stand in that great and terrible day? Is any of us worthy? Let not fear engulf your heart. Jesus wants to remind you that His grace is sufficient for you and me. Those with clean hands and pureness of heart will be able to stand. You have reasons to shout and praise the Lamb of God that takes away the sin of the world.

Heavenly Father, we pray for the day when we shall see Jesus face to face and joy shall fill our hearts forever. We ask that by the power of your Holy Spirit, we will develop the gentle character of Christ. May our thoughts and hearts be pure so we may stand before the presence of a holy God. We ask this in Jesus's name, amen.

Reflections, Thoughts, and Prayer

_____

_____

_____

_____

_____

_____

_____

April 24

In the world ye shall have tribulation: but be of
good cheer; I have overcome the world.
—John 16:33 (KJV)

When we think of what the disciples went through to spread the good news, that alone should strengthen our faith. There aren't too many people willing to die for what they believe. However, the disciples had experienced a point of no return with their Redeemer. It was their greatest honor to proclaim Jesus was risen. At every turn of his ministry, Paul was beaten and thrown in jail; he endured many hardships and was perplexed and persecuted. In spite of enemies to his left and right, Paul went on singing because he knew in whom he believed.

Heavenly Father, we pray for an attitude of perseverance especially when it is darkest in our lives. Because we know Jesus lives and has overcome the world, we have nothing to fear, not even death. May we learn from those who have come before us and do our part in this world's history by the leading of your divine Spirit. We ask this in Jesus's name, amen.

Reflections, Thoughts, and Prayer

April 25

For as he thinketh in his heart, so is he.
—Proverbs 23:7 (KJV)

What you allow to enter your mind can bring much joy or suffering. Negative thinking is detrimental to your health. It is every Christian's duty to think on all that is lovely and pure. If you struggle in that area of your life, ask God for His Holy Spirit. He will not turn you away empty.

Heavenly Father, you have asked us to dwell on all things that are true, lovely, honest, pure, and of good report because you desire us to have good lives. At times when we meditate on the wrong thing, we suffer immensely and cause ourselves unnecessary pain. Today, I pray your Holy Spirit will come into our hearts and help us develop the habit of thinking correct thoughts. We pray this in Jesus's name, amen.

Reflections, Thoughts, and Prayer

_____

_____

_____

_____

_____

_____

April 26

The Spirit of the Lord GOD is upon me; because
the LORD hath anointed me to preach good tidings
unto the meek; he hath sent me to bind up the
brokenhearted, to proclaim liberty to the captives, and
the opening of the prison to them that are bound.
—Isaiah 61:1 (KJV)

The world is filled with pain and suffering. All around you can feel the sorrow and hear the woes. It is our place to help alleviate the hardships and bring an end to the misery of those within our reach. Feeding and clothing them will have a greater impact than any sermon we could preach. However, after we have met their physical needs, we need to meet the needs of their souls, which only Christ can fill.

Loving Father, you have blessed us with so much to be a blessing to others in need. We pray we may do the practical part as we lift up your Son, Jesus, amen.

Reflections, Thoughts, and Prayer

April 27

Is there no balm in Gilead; is there no
physician there? Why then is not the health
of the daughter of my people recovered?
—Jeremiah 8:22 (KJV)

*Y*ou are the light of the world. Let your light so shine for Jesus. Many are looking for that light to shine so they may see the glory of God. Many are hopeless, and their faith has gone dim. Speak the Word to them and bring back the sunshine to them. Speak words of courage and cheer. Pray for them and pray with them. Many are hungry for the Bread of life. Study with them. When the soul is sick, only Jesus can do the healing.

Heavenly Father, today, we lift up those who have lost hope and are discouraged. We pray today that through us, they will have an encounter with Christ. We ask for healing, which can come only from above. And we are assured that those you set free are free indeed, amen.

Reflections, Thoughts, and Prayer

April 28

Preach the word; be instant in season, out of season;
reprove, rebuke, exhort with all longsuffering and doctrine.
—2 Timothy 4:2 (KJV)

If we work to create an excitement of feeling, we shall have all we want and more than we can possibly know how to manage. Calmly and clearly "Preach the Word." We must not regard it as our work to create an excitement. The Holy Spirit of God alone can create a healthy enthusiasm. Let God work, and let the human agent walk softly before Him, watching, waiting, praying, looking unto Jesus every moment. (Selected Messages 2:16, 17; 1894)

*H*eavenly Father, we ask that the sermon on how we live our lives will bring about much fruit for your kingdom. Let our action be one of love, hope, and peace. Give us clean hearts so we may reach our fellowmen we pray, amen.

Reflections, Thoughts, and Prayer

_____

_____

_____

_____

_____

April 29

But there were false prophets also among the people, even
as there shall be false teachers among you, who privily shall
bring in damnable heresies, even denying the Lord that
bought them, and bring upon themselves swift destruction.
—2 Peter 2:1 (KJV)

We are living in a time when deception of every kind is all about. This is the time to stand firm on the Word of God. Let not one word be removed or added from what has been written under the inspiration of the Holy Spirit.

Heavenly Father, we ask for guidance from your Holy Spirit to give us a strong foundation in your Word so we will stand firm as deception runs to and fro. May we take time to study is our prayer in Jesus's name, amen.

Reflections, Thoughts, and Prayer

_____

_____

_____

_____

_____

_____

_____

April 30

It is better to trust in the LORD than to put
confidence in man.
—Psalm 118:8 (KJV)

We are to trust Jesus and bring our burdens to Him. How disappointing it is when trials come and we seek our neighbors before seeking Jesus. What can our friends do for us? Can they take away the pain and show us a better way when they are not even able to manage their own burdens? Only Jesus can carry our loads. Trust Him with your cares and He will not disappoint you. He should be the first one you come to in your moment of need. Make Him your confidant.

Heavenly Father, we put our trust in you. We cannot help ourselves. We ask for a portion of your Holy Spirit to abide in us so we may have a love for spiritual matters. We pray in Jesus's name, amen.

Reflections, Thoughts, and Prayer

_____

_____

_____

_____

_____

_____

_____

May 1

Blessed is the man unto whom the LORD imputeth
not iniquity, and in whose spirit there is no guile.
—Psalm 32:2 (KJV)

We should all strive to be among the 144,000. We should pray for a burden to help others gain heaven as well. Christ died so we might live. We should make it a duty to study His life daily. We will gain much to understand how He was tempted in all points but did not sin so the universe could see that all who truly want to can live lives pleasing to God.

Heavenly Father, I pray for a new heart of love for others so I can tell them of your great love. I pray for strength from your Holy Spirit to be among the hundred and forty-four thousand. Make this life you have blessed me with a useful one for your kingdom I pray in Jesus's name, amen.

Reflections, Thoughts, and Prayer

_____

_____

_____

_____

_____

_____

May 2

> Then shall the kingdom of heaven be likened unto
> ten virgins, which took their lamps, and went forth
> to meet the bridegroom. They that were foolish took
> their lamps, and took no oil with them: But the
> wise took oil in their vessels with their lamps.
> —Matthew 25:1, 3–4 (KJV)

*N*ow is the time to build a character fit for heaven. When Jesus returns, it will be too late to make changes in wrong habits. Only you with the help of His Spirit can do this work. This oil is nontransferable.

Loving Father, we ask for a character pleasing to you. We desire to be like the ten wise virgins with plenty of oil in our lamps. Work with us and in us by the power of your Holy Spirit we pray, amen.

Reflections, Thoughts, and Prayer

_____

_____

_____

_____

_____

_____

_____

_____

May 3

Obey those who rule over you, and be submissive,
for they watch out for your souls, as those who must
give account. Let them do so with joy and not with
grief, for that would be unprofitable for you.
—Hebrews 13:17 (KJV)

We are to submit to those in authority. We should show respect for the work they do and see how we can be a source of support and not hindrance. However, this is as long as it is in harmony with what God has said in His Word. God is our supreme leader. If those in charge are contradicting the Word of God, it is best to follow God. Stand firm on His principles.

Our allegiance is to you, O Lord. Help us live in harmony with your laws. We pray for our leaders, and we ask your will be done though them as well as through us, amen.

Reflections, Thoughts, and Prayer

_____

_____

_____

_____

_____

_____

May 4

I am my beloved's, and my beloved is mine.
—Song of Solomon 6:3 (KJV)

We should aim to love as Christ loved. That means to think of others at all times and in all places and think how we can help ease their pain, bring comfort, make peace, and spread the love of Christ. Learning to smile more, speaking words of kindness, and being pleasant and gentle in mannerisms. These cost nothing to give, but they have such an impact on the receiver as well as the giver. Others will yearn to be in our surroundings because they will have a sense we have been with Jesus.

Heavenly Father, we pray for a loving spirit, one that will display kindness and love by our actions. May that pleasant fragrance surrounds us in every relationship we cultivate; that is our prayer in Jesus's name, amen.

Reflections, Thoughts, and Prayer

_____

_____

_____

_____

_____

_____

_____

May 5

And David danced before the LORD with all his might.
—2 Samuel 6:14 (KJV)

David's dancing in reverent joy before God has been cited by pleasure lovers in justification of the fashionable modern dance, but there is no ground for such an argument. In our day dancing is associated with folly and midnight reveling. Health and morals are sacrificed to pleasure. By the frequenters of the ballroom God is not an object of thought and reverence; prayer or the song of praise would be felt to be out of place in their assemblies. (AH 517.1)

We pray we will learn how to be more Christlike in all we do. May we be more reverent, joyful, peaceful, and loving. Cultivate a right spirit within us we ask in Jesus's name, amen.

Reflections, Thoughts, and Prayer

_____

_____

_____

_____

_____

May 6

If any of you lack wisdom, let him ask of
God, that giveth to all men liberally, and
upbraideth not; and it shall be given him.
—James 1:5 (KJV)

Daily surrendering to God is the only way we can get closer to understanding His way. Ask for His Holy Spirit to come into your heart.

Heavenly Father, we pray for your Holy Spirit to descend on us. We ask for wisdom because we recognize the state we are in. Precious gems are in your holy Word that we do not understand because of our lack of understanding. We pray for a tender heart and a loving nature knowing that through Christ, all things are possible, amen.

Reflections, Thoughts, and Prayer

_____

_____

_____

_____

_____

_____

_____

May 7

Even as the Son of man came not to be ministered unto,
but to minister, and to give his life a ransom for many.
—Matthew 20:28 (KJV)

There is an unceasing amount of reward in service. Doing something for others when they least expect it could bring many tears of joy to the receiver. Service opens the door to witness to others. Christ served the people by meeting their needs; those who had received the blessing were more than willing to proclaim what the Lord had done. Go and tell it to the world in service.

We are called to follow the example of our elder brother, Jesus Christ. We pray we will minister to others as we strengthen ourselves in the word, amen.

Reflections, Thoughts, and Prayer

_____

_____

_____

_____

_____

_____

_____

May 8

That in the ages to come he might shew the
exceeding riches of his grace in his kindness
toward us through Christ Jesus.
—Ephesians 2:7 (KJV)

God has an unlimited amount of ways to care for you. Look at all He's created; it's perfect, and it's never ending. Every day, new planets are being discovered and the universe seems to be stretching wider and longer. Hope for the best. Dream the biggest dream you can and God will match it with an even bigger reality.

Heavenly Father, we know you have blessed us so we may be a blessing to others. We continue to pray for guidance so we cease wasting time and begin to make an impact on the lives of those around us. Give us a new vision on how to accomplish your will for our lives; we ask this in the matchless name of Jesus, amen.

Reflections, Thoughts, and Prayer

_____

_____

_____

_____

_____

_____

May 9

And in his temple doth every one speak of his glory.
—Psalm 29:9 (KJV)

When the enemy attacks like a roaring lion, do not speak of what he has done and his power but of what God is doing; speak of God's power. Remember that the glory belongs to God. At all times, He should be lifted up. Glorify God even in the darkest times of your life. Lift Him up! He is worthy!

Heavenly Father, we want to talk of your goodness. We want to praise you for being a great God, a great Father. We pray that when the shadows of life are cast our way, we will uplift the Man, Christ Jesus. Help us talk faith until all shadows dissipate. We ask this in Jesus's name, amen.

Reflections, Thoughts, and Prayer

_____

_____

_____

_____

_____

_____

_____

May 10

Who shall not fear thee, O Lord, and glorify thy name?
For thou only art holy: for all nations shall come and
worship before thee; for thy judgments are made manifest.
—Revelation 15:4 (KJV)

The day is fast approaching that even those who deny your existence will confess that you are God, holy and true. Satan stirred up much rebellion in heaven, but he too will bow in adoration soon, show you respect and glory, and give you the praise that has been due to you since creation. Who shall not fear you when you are so holy, pure, and loving? Who shall not glorify your name when you are so mighty in battle?

A day is soon approaching where even Satan will declare once and for all you are the one and only fair and righteous God. Let everyone glorify your Holy name today giving thanks to Jesus, amen.

Reflections, Thoughts, and Prayer

_____

_____

_____

_____

_____

_____

_____

May 11

Beloved, now are we the sons of God, and it doth not yet
appear what we shall be: but we know that, when he shall
appear, we shall be like him; for we shall see him as he is.
—1 John 3:2 (KJV)

*L*et us talk of our beloved Savior as John the disciple did. Talk of
His love, talk of His sacrifice, and talk of His grace. Let us reflect
Christ's attributes in our own characters.

Be all that Christ would be. Be patient, be kind, be compassionate,
and be merciful and quick to forgive. Jesus loves those who raise the
banner of God high. He loves those who represent His Father's image.
One day, we shall see our Savior face to face when we will be with Him
throughout eternity.

Heavenly Father, we pray today we will represent you and others
through us will see your beauty and experience your love. May our desire
is to be more like Jesus we pray, amen.

Reflections, Thoughts, and Prayer

_____

_____

_____

_____

_____

_____

May 12

> For the LORD shall comfort Zion: he will comfort
> all her waste places; and he will make her wilderness
> like Eden, and her desert like the garden of the
> LORD; joy and gladness shall be found therein,
> thanksgiving, and the voice of melody.
> —Isaiah 51:3 (KJV)

We are living the final moments of earth's history. It is time to put away sin and put on the whole armor of God. Ask God to set you free from whatever is keeping you under the chains of bondage. Search your heart, and allow God to remove all the bitterness of sin and fill you with zeal to tell of Christ's soon return.

Heavenly Father, we await that day when you shall comfort us and we will be with Jesus forever. Oh what a day to behold. Create in us a new heart; that is our prayer in Jesus's name, amen.

Reflections, Thoughts, and Prayer

_____

_____

_____

_____

_____

_____

May 13

Now the God of hope fill you with all joy and
peace in believing, that ye may abound in hope,
through the power of the Holy Ghost.
—Romans 15:13 (KJV)

Before the coming of Christ, we are told in Holy Scripture of some fundamental events that are to take place. The apostle asked in 2 Thessalonians 2:2, "That you be not soon shaken in mind, or be troubled, neither by spirit, nor by word, nor by letter as from us, as that the day of Christ is at hand."

Now is the time to pray for God's Holy Spirit to give us strength to endure as children whose hope is in the Almighty. This is the time to watch prophecies unfold and pray that your faith will not be shaken or stirred.

Heavenly Father, thank you for revealing to us just how the story of this world will play out. We know that troublous times are ahead, but our hearts can go on singing because of whose we are, amen.

Reflections, Thoughts, and Prayer

_____

_____

_____

_____

_____

_____

May 14

Who is like unto thee, O LORD, among the gods?
Who is like thee, glorious in holiness,
fearful in praises, doing wonders?
—Exodus 15:11 (KJV)

God is constantly working behind the scenes of our lives. He is ever gently directing our paths and taking us to higher grounds as long as we choose to allow Him to work with us. Just look around you. Everything testifies of His love for you and me. Pray big and expect even bigger blessings. Mediocre is not part of God's vocabulary.

Yes Lord, we will trust you during sunny days as well as during the stormy days of our lives because we cannot think of anyone with the mercy, power, and grace you have. We will praise you because we are limited. We know that if you are for us, who dare be against us? Amen.

Reflections, Thoughts, and Prayer

_____

_____

_____

_____

_____

_____

_____

May 15

Ask, and it shall be given you; seek, and ye shall
find; knock, and it shall be opened unto you.
—Matthew 7:7 (KJV)

*I*f God said it, you must believe it. There is so much deception and darkness lurking around that you have to seek the Lord in solitude. He will reveal to you great and marvelous things. He will not turn you away if you knock. He is ready to open the door to let you in. Remember that he fashioned you with His hands. Oh how He loves you and me.

Heavenly Father, here we are asking for us to do our part in these end times so the work may finish and we may go home to the New Jerusalem. That you will feed us so we may feed others we pray in Jesus's name, amen.

Reflections, Thoughts, and Prayer

_____

_____

_____

_____

_____

_____

_____

May 16

> But he answered nothing.
> —Mark 15:3 (KJV)

There is no spectacle in all the Bible so sublime as the silent Savior answering not a word to the men who were maligning Him, and whom He could have laid prostrate at His feet by one look of Divine power, or one word of fiery rebuke. But He let them say and do their worst, and He stood in the power of stillness-God's holy silent Lamb. There is a stillness that lets God work for us, and holds our peace. (SD 3/18)

*H*eavenly Father, there are times when we should follow the Savior's example and keep quiet. We know that when we are still, you are working it out for our good. We give you thanks for the blood of the Lamb and all He endured so we may be victorious, amen.

Reflections, Thoughts, and Prayer

_____

_____

_____

_____

_____

_____

May 17

But wilt thou know, O vain man, that faith
without works is dead?
—James 2:20 (KJV)

A Christian is constantly on duty. There is no time to be idle. Inactivity cripples the soul and depresses the spirit. Seeking the lost should be our first priority. Our lives should be useful and helpful.

Heavenly Father, we give you thanks that we are able to believe and exercise our faith. May we live what we believe so the Jesus in us will draw all humanity to you and to eternal life. We pray for favor to act in Jesus's name, amen.

Reflections, Thoughts, and Prayer

_____

_____

_____

_____

_____

_____

_____

May 18

Be still, and know that I am God.
—Psalm 46:10 (KJV)

*M*oses assured God's children in Exodus 14:13 to fear not, stand still, and see the salvation of the Lord, which he will show to you today; for the Egyptians whom you have seen today, you shall see them no more. When tribulations come rearing their ugly heads is the time to pray to be still and know God is already there fighting for you.

Heavenly Father, as your children, we know nothing happens to us by accident because you are leading us. When the trials of life come, may we learn to be still and allow you to fight for us because we are no match for the enemy alone. We give you thanks for being all powerful in our lives, amen.

Reflections, Thoughts, and Prayer

_____

_____

_____

_____

_____

_____

_____

May 19

Casting all your care upon him, for he careth for you.
—1 Peter 5:7 (KJV)

God's heart is toward you. You are the apple of His eye. Talk to Him. Tell Him all about your day, your wants, you needs, your joys, and your fears. Tell Him what you're struggling with and what you're hoping for. He is faithful and will not fail you.

Heavenly Father, I cast all my cares on you. The burdens of life can be too much for me, but I know you are here with me and you care for me. I trust your leading in Jesus's name, amen.

Reflections, Thoughts, and Prayer

May 20

He that is slow to anger is better than the mighty; and
he that ruleth his spirit than he that taketh a city.
—Proverbs 16:32 (KJV)

It's easy to be on one's best behavior when everything is going well, but does your spirit throw a tantrum when you're not getting your way? Let God's Holy Spirit work on you to be at peace even in the darkest hour of your life.

Heavenly Father, we ask for your Holy Spirit to give us strength to overcome self—our greatest enemy. O Father, we are in need of you today. We ask this in Jesus's name, amen.

Reflections, Thoughts, and Prayer

_____

_____

_____

_____

_____

_____

_____

_____

_____

May 21

But the LORD was with Joseph, and shewed him mercy,
and gave him favour in the sight of the
keeper of the prison.
—Genesis 39:21 (KJV)

Like Joseph, let us be more careful to learn all the
lessons in the school of sorrow than we are anxious
for the hour of deliverance. There is a "need –be" for
every lesson, and when we are ready, our deliverance
will surely come, and we shall find that we could not
have stood in our place of higher service withoug the
very things that were taught us in the ordeal. God is
educating us for the future, for higher service and noble
blessings. (Selected S/D)

The trying times are difficult indeed. But may we learn from Joseph
and allow you to polish us and lead us always, amen.

Reflections, Thoughts, and Prayer

_____

_____

_____

_____

_____

_____

May 22

The LORD is my shepherd: I shall not want.
—Psalm 23:1 (KJV)

When we think of a shepherd, we think of someone who tends to a flock. So it is with Christ, the Good Shepherd. He is always looking to do us good. He protects our goings and comings. He looks for ways to bless us. He never sleeps or slumbers. His constant gaze is on us, His beloved children. We can rest assured that all our provisions have been made and we shall want for nothing.

Heavenly Father, why do we doubt your goodness and your love? Today, I ask for forgiveness and surrender this heart to you. You have met all my needs, and I know I will want for nothing because you are the Good Shepherd in whom my trust is, amen.

Reflections, Thoughts, and Prayer

_____

_____

_____

_____

_____

_____

_____

May 23

For his merciful kindness is great toward us: and the truth
of the LORD endureth for ever. Praise ye the LORD.
—Psalm 117:2 (KJV)

*W*hen we praise and meditate on God's love, our downcast spirits
are lifted and joy comes flooding through our beings again. It
is healthy to meditate daily. Think of how merciful God is. Think of
His many blessings. Think of His wondrous love. Praise Him morning,
noon, and night.

Heavenly Father, thank you for your loving thoughts toward us.
Help us to talk more of your goodness and less of our trials trusting
that if you allowed them, we can handle them by the power of your
Holy Spirit, amen.

Reflections, Thoughts, and Prayer

_____

_____

_____

_____

_____

_____

_____

May 24

Fight the good fight of faith.
—1 Timothy 6:12 (KJV)

Faith is what we need to fight these ominous times as earth's history is soon to end. It will be a most difficult fight, but let me encourage you to fight it at any cost because the promises of God are sure, true, and certain. Do not be discouraged; do not lose your faith. Anything you ask, believe and have faith and you will receive it because God's words are yea and amen.

God, I thank you that I can handle everything that comes my way. Thank you for the angels that excel in strength and accompany me through it all. I am putting my hand in your hand, the hand that rules the universe in Jesus's name, amen.

Reflections, Thoughts, and Prayer

_____

_____

_____

_____

_____

_____

_____

May 25

He called to her, and said, Bring me, I pray thee, a
morsel of bread in thine hand. And she said, As the
LORD thy God liveth, I have not a cake, but an
handful of meal in a barrel, and a little oil in a cruse.
—1 King 17:11–12 (KJV)

God is so awesome that He has given everyone something unique
to him or her be it a talent in being hospitable, a gentle soul, or an
intellectual voice. Whatever it may be and no matter how small it is,
use it to give Him glory. When we fail to use what God has given, we
work against Him.

Heavenly Father, may we use our means and our time you have
blessed us with to show others we care. That our lifestyle be one that
seeks to serve we pray in Jesus's name, amen.

Reflections, Thoughts, and Prayer

_____

_____

_____

_____

_____

_____

_____

May 26

> For the which cause I also suffer these things:
> nevertheless I am not ashamed: for I know whom
> I have believed, and am persuaded that he is able
> to keep that which I have committed unto him.
> —2 Timothy 1:12 (KJV)

When the apostles came to a place in their walk with Christ, they were able to say, "I know whom I have believed." Let it be your goal to walk with God to the place where nothing will deter you, nothing will cause your faith to waver, and you too can say the same of your Redeemer.

Loving Father, we want our faith to be fully established in you, nothing wavering. May we know you so intimately that we can say as the apostles did that we know whom we have believed, amen.

Reflections, Thoughts, and Prayer

_____

_____

_____

_____

_____

_____

_____

May 27

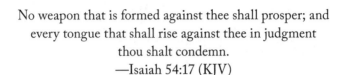

No weapon that is formed against thee shall prosper; and
every tongue that shall rise against thee in judgment
thou shalt condemn.
—Isaiah 54:17 (KJV)

God's promises are true, but we must do our part to remain separate and distinct, to be His peculiar people who do righteousness. God will be our shield, our defense, and protector, and no weapon formed against us shall prosper.

What beautiful words these are that your blood covers us and that no weapon formed against us shall prosper. Help us be the peculiar people you have called us to be in Jesus's name, amen.

Reflections, Thoughts, and Prayer

_____

_____

_____

_____

_____

_____

_____

_____

May 28

And the serpent said unto the woman,
ye shall not surely die.
—Genesis 3:4 (KJV)

There are times when you can see the tempter coming a mile away. Rebuke his temptations with the almighty Word of God and he will flee from you. Do not allow doubt or darkness to set in. Do not open the door to his temptations.

We give you thanks, loving Father, for Your Word. We can meditate on all your promises and cautions. Help us keep our minds on you so we may never find ourselves in a situation in which we have to doubt you. Give us your Spirit; we ask this in Jesus's name, amen.

Reflections, Thoughts, and Prayer

_____

_____

_____

_____

_____

_____

_____

May 29

> But this one thing I do, forgetting those things which are
> behind, and reaching forth unto those things
> which are before.
> —Philippians 3:13 (KJV)

*N*o matter how busy your life gets, never lose sight of the one great purpose, that one desire that God has put in your heart. Press toward your mark.

Heavenly Father, we are thankful to have the power through your Holy Spirit to let go of the disappointments, self-pity, and broken dreams and break free from all the deadness in our lives and know you have so much better in store for us in our future. With Jesus in the vessel, we can smile at the storm and press toward our high callings in Jesus's name, amen.

Reflections, Thoughts, and Prayer

_____

_____

_____

_____

_____

_____

_____

May 30

And the LORD said unto Samuel,
How long wilt thou mourn for Saul.
—1 Samuel 16:1 (KJV)

When trouble and difficulties come, we are ready to accuse God telling of how He has neglected or failed us. If in His mercy, He sees fit to cut off whatever it may be, we mourn without stopping to think that our loving God is working it all out for our own good.

God, we sometimes don't know why something was taken away or didn't come to pass, but we will still trust you because you are on the throne. Help us have a season of mourning but to move forward holding your hand. We believe you are working it out for our good. Thank you for being a loving Father, amen.

Reflections, Thoughts, and Prayer

_____

_____

_____

_____

_____

_____

_____

_____

May 31

He is not here: for he is risen, as he said.
—Matthew 28:6 (KJV)

Tell of the marvelous life of Jesus Christ. Tell of how He lived a life of praying, healing, and teaching. Tell of His brutal and painful death. How the sins of all those who lived, are living, and will live were on His shoulders. Tell of how He conquered death by rising on the third day just as He had said.

Heavenly Father, we rejoice today because we have resurrection power; Jesus conquered all sin on the cross. We can embrace our future with gladness and hope. Death has no power over you, almighty God. We pray for power from on high in Jesus's name, amen.

Reflections, Thoughts, and Prayer

_____

_____

_____

_____

_____

_____

_____

_____

June 1

Not by might, nor by power, but by my spirit,
saith the LORD of hosts.
—Zechariah 4:6 (KJV)

When you decide to work for God to reach others dying in sin, expect to meet with persecution and maltreatment. Look at the examples of the disciples; they rejoiced that they were called to suffer for Christ. They didn't focus on their inabilities or their weaknesses. They considered it a privilege to work for the Savior. Without worry of what would happen to them, they labored for their Master, and God was able to work through them to reach many, even you and me.

You are a mighty God, and when we come to know you as the disciples did, we will consider it an honor to know you and be used by you. May we too leave our mark on the historical pages of earth's final days; we pray this in Jesus's name, amen.

Reflections, Thoughts, and Prayer

_____

_____

_____

_____

_____

_____

June 2

> And the child grew, and she brought him unto Pharaoh's
> daughter, and he became her son. And she called his name
> Moses: and she said, Because I drew him out of water.
> —Exodus 2:10 (KJV)

God is working behind the scenes of our lives. Keep your peace and stay faithful. After you have done all you can, stand still and know He is God.

Heavenly Father, help us take you at your word. Just as you delivered Moses as a baby to Pharaoh's daughter when the decree went out that all baby boys had to be put to death and allowed Moses' biological mother to be paid to raise him, why do we continue to doubt you? I believe you are able to open doors and line up the right people to bless us in order to bless others. Increase our faith we pray, amen.

Reflections, Thoughts, and Prayer

_____

_____

_____

_____

_____

_____

_____

June 3

And she answered, It is well.
—2 Kings 4:26 (KJV)

The true measure of our character is not how we react when all is well but how we react when all is not well, when everything we have worked for has come tumbling down. If we are able to remain in the love of God with the assurance all is well though all does not look well, we are fit to be called Christians.

Heavenly Father, we do *not* like the trials this life brings, but like the Shunammite woman, may we learn to say it is well as we make our way to your throne room on our knees in prayer knowing that with you, it is all well. That we may we trust you in the darkness as we do in the light, we pray in Jesus's name, amen.

Reflections, Thoughts, and Prayer

_____

_____

_____

_____

_____

_____

_____

June 4

> And he saith unto them, Why are ye fearful, O
> ye of little faith? Then he arose, and rebuked the
> winds and the sea; and there was a great calm.
> —Matthew 8:26 (KJV)

I can picture how the disciples' boat was being tossed by the boisterous waves. Those rugged fishermen were skilled in stormy situations, but this storm was one they had not foreseen; it was one they had not yet encountered. They were trying everything they could to save themselves and forgot Jesus was in their midst.

Have we forgotten that you are on the ship of life with us, dear Father? Have we forgotten we are children of the Living God? Please forgive us. We pray you will calm the storms in our lives for Christ's sake, amen.

Reflections, Thoughts, and Prayer

_____

_____

_____

_____

_____

_____

_____

June 5

But when he saw the wind boisterous, he was afraid; and
beginning to sink, he cried, saying, "Lord, save me."
—Matthew 14:30 (KJV)

*P*eter loved Jesus. When he told Jesus he would never betray Him, Peter meant it. Peter was willing to follow Jesus even to death, but Peter did not know that in his heart were weeds of evil that could come to light only in the most difficult trials. Peter was tried, and he came to a place that he knew he was entirely dependent on God. We must learn from Peter to have faith in God totally because only He can save us.

Like Peter, I recognize I need to distrust myself and have an increased faith in Christ. Please save me from myself, O Father, I pray, amen.

Reflections, Thoughts, and Prayer

_____

_____

_____

_____

_____

_____

_____

_____

June 6

The next day John seeth Jesus coming unto him, and saith,
Behold the Lamb of God, which taketh
away the sin of the world.
—John 1:29 (KJV)

*I*t was a custom to go to Jerusalem to offer up a goat, dove, and lamb for a sin offering. These offerings were to be perfect and spotless for they foreshadowed Jesus Christ, who was to come as the Lamb of God to die once and for all.

Heavenly Father, we can't thank you enough for the gift of your only Son, Jesus. Once and for all, he made His way to the treacherous road to Calvary carrying the sins of the world on His shoulders. He conquered death victoriously and paid the price of sin fully once and for all. It is in His name we pray, amen.

Reflections, Thoughts, and Prayer

_____

_____

_____

_____

_____

_____

_____

June 7

These are they which came out of great
tribulation, and have washed their robes, and
made them white in the blood of the Lamb.
—Revelation 7:14 (KJV)

*I*t should be the prayer of us all to be among those who have been washed by the blood of the Lamb. Do not think that it is too late for you or that you are too far gone to return home to Jesus. He can make your sin-stained robe white again.

Heavenly Father, we are not afraid of trials because you are the Ruler of this vast universe and our lives. You have told us how this will all end through scripture. Father, we have our eyes fixed on Jesus, our Savior, because we know we will come out of great tribulation into great jubilation for we have been redeemed by the blood of Christ, the Lamb, amen.

Reflections, Thoughts, and Prayer

_____

_____

_____

_____

_____

_____

_____

June 8

And, behold, a woman, which was diseased
with an issue of blood twelve years, came behind
him, and touched the hem of his garment.
—Matthew 9:20 (KJV)

Jesus was surrounded by so many when the woman with the issue of blood reached to touch the hem of His garment and was instantly healed. I wonder how many in the multitude were sick but not healed. What made the difference for the woman? Faith.

Loving Lord, I need the touch of living faith. I'm tired of the routine that leaves me powerless and having just the form of godliness. I want to be like the woman with the issue of blood and know that if I could just touch the hem of Christ's hem, I too would be made whole. You did it for her, and I know you can do it for me, amen.

Reflections, Thoughts, and Prayer

_____

_____

_____

_____

_____

_____

_____

June 9

> The other disciples therefore said unto him, we
> have seen the Lord. But he said unto them, except
> I shall see in his hands the print of the nails, and
> put my finger into the print of the nails, and thrust
> my hand into his side, I will not believe.
> —John 20:25 (KJV)

We are in need of more faith. We say we believe, and yet we question every turn that doesn't add up to our understanding. If we had that unwavering faith, we would take God at His word and believe all He has promised. This is faith.

Loving Father, you are working in the lives of others around us. People have fresh testimonies of your goodness and kindness. Are we like Thomas? Not believing until we see? Please take away our doubts so we too may glorify your name, amen.

Reflections, Thoughts, and Prayer

_____

_____

_____

_____

_____

_____

_____

June 10

Then saith he to Thomas, Reach hither thy finger, and
behold my hands; and reach hither thy hand, and thrust
it into my side: and be not faithless, but believing.
—John 20:27 (KJV)

*J*esus's example of how He came to doubting Thomas should be an
example to us on how we ought to treat those precious souls who
have doubt. In His loving and gentle nature, Christ allowed Thomas to
see He had indeed risen from the grave. He did not rebuke Thomas or
start a debate with him; He revealed Himself to Thomas.

What a tender and compassionate Father you are because you do
not treat us as we deserve but like royalty. We thank you for your love.
May we learn from you daily, amen.

Reflections, Thoughts, and Prayer

_____

_____

_____

_____

_____

_____

_____

June 11

> But I know, that even now, whatsoever thou
> wilt ask of God, God will give it thee.
> —John 11:22 (KJV)

*S*ome love to put a spin on God's Word, but it is clear that whatever you ask of God, He will give it. I think of Martha and how she ran to Jesus to tell Him Lazarus had died four days earlier. She told Him He was four days too late. But Martha knew that whatever Jesus asked of His Father, He would receive. Even so today, when we ask in Jesus's name, we will receive.

Heavenly Father, like Martha, we believe that even now, you can turn our situation around. Even now, we can be healed. Even now, our finances can turn around for the good. Even now, our dreams can come true. Turn things around for us even now we pray in Jesus's name, amen.

Reflections, Thoughts, and Prayer

_____

_____

_____

_____

_____

_____

_____

June 12

Thou shalt call, and I will answer thee.
—Job 14:15 (KJV)

When trials come to assail your soul and take away your peace, that is the time to cry out to God. God allows crises in your life so you may know only He has the power to take it away and to heal. Some burdens are so heavy that only God can carry them. God wants you to look to Him alone. God will be there when you call on Him; He will answer. He is ever ready to fulfill His promises. Call on Him. Trust His leading.

Heavenly Father, we are claiming this promise that when we call, you will answer. Help us not to simply talk about prayer but to pray, amen.

Reflections, Thoughts, and Prayer

_____

_____

_____

_____

_____

_____

_____

June 13

O Lord, how long shall I cry, and thou wilt not hear!
—Habakkuk 1:2 (KJV)

To those who have been praying for some time now with no visible result in sight, I implore you to keep on praying. Press your petitions before the throne of God. Persevere in prayer as Hannah and Daniel did. Believe that your answer is on its way. God is too good to be unkind. Trust and praise Him.

Loving Father, we have waited a long time for Jesus to come. We see prophecies fulfilling. We know these are the final days of earth's history. Like Habakkuk, there are days when we feel our prayers are not reaching heaven, but keep us faithful nonetheless because we know you are in control. We continue to pray and wait with praises and thanksgiving, amen.

Reflections, Thoughts, and Prayer

_____

_____

_____

_____

_____

_____

June 14

Come now, and let us reason together, saith the LORD.
—Isaiah 1:18 (KJV)

God has invited us to reason together with Him. God's Word is simple, but some fail to accept it as it is because people have put their interpretations on it so they can live as they want and do what is contradictory to the Word of God. For this reason, some prefer to follow false doctrines.

Heavenly Father, we accept the invitation given to us to come and reason together. There are times when we have questions only you can answer, and we seek to know your will for our lives as well as ask you plainly to reveal to us what we ought to pray for. But most important, we need your Holy Spirit to help us know and understand your way for Christ's sake, amen.

Reflections, Thoughts, and Prayer

_____

_____

_____

_____

_____

_____

June 15

And with your feet fitted with the readiness
that comes from the gospel of peace.
—Ephesians 6:15 (KJV)

We must stay in the Word. Daily study of scripture is necessary to share with those who need hope. When we fail to study, we have very little to offer. We present the Word in our own words and strength instead of speaking in the power of God's Holy Spirit. The Word of God will bring about reform; it will not aggravate the hearer. The Word should be in presented in love.

Heavenly Father, today, we pray we will put on our shoes of peace and shake off the offenses that might come our way. We ask that our lips be seasoned with love and peace from on high to draw others to you, amen.

Reflections, Thoughts, and Prayer

_____

_____

_____

_____

_____

_____

_____

June 16

Without being frightened in any way by those who oppose
you. This is a sign to them that they will be destroyed.
—Philippians 1:28 (KJV)

*Y*ou are more precious to God than you realize. There is no need to
go through life with a depressed, downcast spirit. Every promise
in the gospel is made for you to claim. You are not an outcast no matter
how dark your path may have been. Give your burdens to Christ. Once
you asked for forgiveness, God forgave you. No need to afflict your soul
as Martin Luther did his. Remember, Jesus died so you could live.

Heavenly Father, we will not be afraid of any obstacle for we know
you, the greatest force in the universe, are for us and on our side. We are
leaving all our health, financial, and relationship issues in your hands,
and it is a good day today, amen.

Reflections, Thoughts, and Prayer

_____

_____

_____

_____

_____

_____

_____

June 17

In all thy ways acknowledge him,
and he shall direct thy paths.
—Proverbs 3:6 (KJV)

*B*elieve that Jesus loves you. Trust Him in all you do. Patiently wait on Him. He will open doors to new and better opportunities. Some may say what they will, others may believe what they will, but I pray you will believe in God's many blessings He has for your life. Believe in the Lord. That is true evidence of being a Christian.

Heavenly Father, we want to acknowledge you in everything before us great or small. We know you want to be involved in the intricate details of our lives, and we are in need of your guidance. We put this day before you—our families, friends, our goings and comings. We pray for unlimited favor in Jesus's name, amen.

Reflections, Thoughts, and Prayer

_____

_____

_____

_____

_____

_____

_____

June 18

And the LORD shall make thee the head,
and not the tail; and thou shalt be above only,
and thou shalt not be beneath.
—Deuteronomy 28:13 (KJV)

The Nike slogan "just do it" is true for everyone whose goal in life is to be successful. Keep your goal in view, and pray for God to multiply your efforts. You must think about what you want to be and go and be it!

Heavenly Father, we thank you for the assurance that as your children, we are the head, not the tail—that we shall be above, not beneath. We know you are guiding our feet with every step we take. If we could only see how you are working things out for our good, we would trust you. Help us know your will for our lives on earth so that may be our aim; we pray this in Jesus's name, amen.

Reflections, Thoughts, and Prayer

_____

_____

_____

_____

_____

_____

_____

June 19

> And God said, Let us make man in our image,
> after our likeness.
> —Genesis 1:26 (KJV)

When God made us in His image, He had the highest level of accomplishments for us to attain. Because of sin, we have been crippled from generation to generation. God still wants us to reach our full potential. He knows what we can become if we submit to Him. With divine intervention, we are full of capabilities we are not aware of. We should not limit God or ourselves.

Heavenly Father, we are thankful we are made in your image. We pray for new vision and goals for our lives knowing that as we connect with you, we will accomplish those goals. We don't want to go to our graves with undeveloped or unfulfilled dreams, unsung songs, or unwritten books; we want to excel wherever you have placed us for your glory, amen.

Reflections, Thoughts, and Prayer

_____

_____

_____

_____

_____

June 20

And the LORD said unto Satan, Behold, all that he hath
is in thy power, only upon himself put not
forth thine hand.
—Job 1:12 (KJV)

God is in control. He is controlling everything including the limit sin can reach. Through your prayers, God can limit what the enemy wants to do. I love how Ellen White says even in death, know that your Father's loving hands hold the bitter cup to your lips. Let us never lose faith in God.

Most high God, we give you thanks that all power remains with you. We have nothing to fear because there is a limit the enemy has and that all things occurring need your permission before they can come our way. Keep us faithful we pray, amen.

Reflections, Thoughts, and Prayer

_____

_____

_____

_____

_____

_____

_____

June 21

And the LORD said unto Satan, Hast thou considered
my servant Job, that there is none like him in the earth.
—Job 1:8 (KJV)

We are not to live lives free of troubles and trials. We will all have
burdens to bear, but we are called to believe that no matter what,
God is there. He said, "I am with you always."

Job gave God thanks for the good, and Job blessed God when all
had been taken away from Him. Blessed be the name of the Lord.

Heavenly Father, we should count it a privilege when trials come
knowing you are bragging about us to the enemy, who is not able to
harm us because we are sheltered in the arms of Christ. We pray that
our eyes will always be on you lest we should fall and perish, amen.

Reflections, Thoughts, and Prayer

_____

_____

_____

_____

_____

_____

_____

June 22

Believe in the LORD your God, so shall ye be
established; believe his prophets, so shall ye prosper.
—*2 Chronicles 20:20 (KJV)*

*A*ll heaven is watching to see the kind of faith you have in times of
need. It does your soul good to pray earnestly before starting your
day. Take time to study what the prophets, who were inspired by God's
Holy Spirit, wrote in the Holy Scriptures. When you take the time to
know God in the toughest period of your life, you will know His eyes
are always on you.

As the school year has come to an end, we turn to you, heavenly
Father, to thank you for seeing us through, keeping us safe, and granting
us favor. As summer begins, we pray for a hedge of protection around us,
our children, family, friends, and all those we love. May we take time
to reflect on your goodness and many blessings and cooperate with your
Holy Spirit to build our characters for your kingdom. We pray this in
Jesus's name, amen.

Reflections, Thoughts, and Prayer

_____

_____

_____

_____

_____

June 23

Ye have not chosen me, but I have chosen you, and
ordained you, that ye should go and bring forth fruit.
—John 15:16 (KJV)

*W*e should know who we are in Christ. He has chosen us to use as vessels to reach thousands and thousands. Every day, we come in contact with people; do they see Jesus in us?

You are called to bring forth much fruit. Display the love of Jesus wherever you are. You never know who's watching. You never know who you're reaching.

Loving Father, we are most honored that you would choose frail, weak human beings like us to vindicate your Word. We pray we will rise to the occasion and uplift Christ Jesus by the way we live our lives. We pray for power in Jesus's name, amen.

Reflections, Thoughts, and Prayer

_____

_____

_____

_____

_____

_____

_____

June 24

But as for me and my house, we will serve the LORD.
—Joshua 24:15 (KJV)

Take a decided stand for God. Jesus came to vindicate His Father's Word and show how loving and merciful God is. We too need to stand up to vindicate God's character. As Joshua did, let us clearly be known whose side we are on. Let us serve the Lord with all our heart, mind, and soul.

Heavenly Father, this day, we choose to be on your side—the winning side. We pray for strength to stand up for you because we know the road is not a smooth one, but we have the assurance of being victorious every time because Jesus has conquered it all on Calvary. We put ourselves under your care in Jesus's name, amen.

Reflections, Thoughts, and Prayer

_____

_____

_____

_____

_____

_____

_____

June 25

I am he that liveth, and was dead; and behold,
I am alive for evermore, Amen; and have the keys of
hell and of death.
—Revelation 1:18 (KJV)

Glory be to Jesus, who has risen from the dead. Because of His victory, we too can be victorious. Because of His death, we may live. Jesus died so we would have life and have it more abundantly. To all those who are dying in sin, come to Jesus and receive eternal life so upon His return, wherever He is, you may be also.

Glory to God on high! Father, we thank you that through the blood of the Lamb, we are free. We thank you that the enemy cannot hold the dead in his grasp because Jesus has the keys to death. Today, we rejoice because we know that though we should die, we live when we die in Christ. Hallelujah forever, amen.

Reflections, Thoughts, and Prayer

_____

_____

_____

_____

_____

_____

June 26

Howbeit this kind goeth not out but by prayer and fasting.
—Matthew 17:21 (KJV)

Jesus fasted and prayed because He knew the road to Calvary would not be an easy one to trudge. He needed to be connected with heaven, so He, who came in the nature after humanity had sinned, would be able to endure the greatest challenge this infinite universe would ever witness. Mighty issues were at stake in the conflict between good and evil. He fasted and prayed as should we.

Heavenly Father, we too have deep-rooted issues we battle, but we are reminded by your holy Word that through prayer and fasting, we will connect with the Vine, who overcame all temptations. Guide us to follow your examples even now we pray in Jesus's name, amen.

Reflections, Thoughts, and Prayer

_____

_____

_____

_____

_____

_____

_____

June 27

Fear not, little flock, for it is your Father's
good pleasure to give you the kingdom.
—Luke 12:32 (KJV)

Cooperation between heaven and earth is essential for success to be attained. Yes, God desires to give you every good gift He has in store, but you have to pray, you have to ask, and you have to believe.

The three Hebrew boys, Shadrach, Meshach, and Abed-nego, decided they would not bow down even if God did not deliver them. And God showed up in a mighty way to deliver them from the fiery furnace.

Heavenly Father, we know you want to give us so much more than we can imagine. Help us to sharpen our talents and do our part so we will be ready to seize the opportunity for greater service to you. We pray for Christ's sake, amen.

Reflections, Thoughts, and Prayer

_____

_____

_____

_____

_____

_____

_____

June 28

But where sin abounded, grace did much more abound.
—Romans 5:20 (KJV)

When Adam ate of the forbidden fruit, he did not set out to sin against God; he simply disobeyed what God had told him not to do. Thousands of years later, we are still paying the results of that single sin. Many of us are doing many things that are right, but we continue to disobey what God has asked us. Thank God He loved us so much that He sent His only begotten Son to make a way to save us from the bondage of sin.

Heavenly Father, thank you for your mercy and grace. Thank you that you would stand at nothing to save us wretched as we are. Yes, we do have the example of Adam, but sin is so deeply rooted in our hearts that we fall into it over and over … but grace! Amen.

Reflections, Thoughts, and Prayer

_____

_____

_____

_____

_____

_____

June 29

> And Shem and Japeth took a garment, and laid it upon
> both their shoulders, and went backward, and covered
> the nakedness of their father; and their faces were
> backward, and they saw not their father's nakedness.
> —Genesis 9:23 (KJV)

Sin is the transgression of the law. It dishonors God and deserves to be punished. Jesus came to cover our sins with His blood. In Christ's righteousness, we stand before God covered. We should also learn to cover the shortcomings of those we love. Don't tell others what they did; take it to God in prayer.

Heavenly Father, we thank you for loved ones who cover our weaknesses and shame by being confidants. Thank you for putting them in our lives. Like Noah's sons, may we not expose the faults of others but pray for those who have failed. We pray this in Jesus's name, amen.

Reflections, Thoughts, and Prayer

June 30

A gossip betrays a confidence;
so avoid a man who talks too much.
—Proverbs 20:19 (KJV)

We should keep gossiping lips far from our presence. Anyone who will gossip to you will gossip about you. God is displeased when we find time to talk so incessantly yet we can't find the words to talk to Him. Much talking does nothing for the soul. Talk less. Pray more. Ask God to teach you how to pray. He surely will.

Heavenly Father, I desire to be more like Christ. I pray your Holy Spirit will do a work in me so my lips will be seasoned with encouragement to uplift others who are on this pathway to heaven. Give me such a dislike for gossiping that I will not want to be present when others are involved in gossiping. May heaven be my focus I pray in Jesus's name, amen.

Reflections, Thoughts, and Prayer

_____

_____

_____

_____

_____

_____

July 1

A friend loveth at all times,
and a brother is born for adversity.
—Proverbs 17:17 (KJV)

*E*veryone we associate with has some kind of influence on us. Choose your friends carefully. Pray that those with whom you associate will help propel you to higher grounds. Some friends will help carry your load when you need help; others will add to it and make your load heavier. Pray for wisdom in choosing.

Most kind and loving Father, thank you for those you have placed in my path for such a time as this, people I know I can count on. They will defend my name and honor in times of adversity. Thank you for friends who love at all times and want to see good for me and not evil. As we call each other brother and sister, may we be deserving of that name is my prayer, amen.

Reflections, Thoughts, and Prayer

_____

_____

_____

_____

_____

_____

July 2

> That in the ages to come he might shew the
> exceeding riches of his grace in his kindness
> toward us through Christ Jesus.
> —Ephesians 2:7 (KJV)

God wants to answer your prayers. He wants to see His beloved children content and full of joy. He desires for us to know we are wholly dependent on Him. Go to Him with everything. Don't pray only during the trying times; praise Him in the glorious times. His storage is full of abundant blessings, and He will not hold any good thing from those who walk uprightly.

Jehovah Jirah, you have provided for all you have made. How great you are! I believe this is the age to expect great things for your glory. Let our lives magnify your holy name we ask in Jesus's name, amen.

Reflections, Thoughts, and Prayer

_____

_____

_____

_____

_____

_____

_____

July 3

A man's heart deviseth his way:
but the Lord directeth his steps.
—Proverbs 16:9 (KJV)

It is good to dream, but remember that God also has a plan for your life that is ten times better than anything you could conjure up. He can open doors as long as you walk in His path.

Loving Father, we need your guidance. We know when we stay in faith and trust you, all the opportunities we seek will find us. May we take time to know you and allow you to do for us what only you can do. Increase our faith we ask in Jesus's name, amen.

Reflections, Thoughts, and Prayer

_____

_____

_____

_____

_____

_____

_____

_____

July 4

But his delight is in the law of the Lord; and in
his law doth he meditate day and night.
—Psalm 1:2 (KJV)

*S*tudying the Word of God should be a delight to every soul seeking to grow in Christ. Alas, thousands upon thousands do not seek the Word for hidden treasures. When you take time to study God's holy scriptures prayerfully, you are putting on the armor that will enable you to fight against spirits in dark places.

Loving Father, I am guilty of not spending enough time studying the Word. I ask for the presence of your Holy Spirit to help me develop the desire to study your precious Word day and night. I want to know you will for my life because I know all you do is good. I trust your leading even today, amen.

Reflections, Thoughts, and Prayer

July 5

Let us therefore come boldly unto the throne of
grace that we may obtain mercy, and find grace to
help in time of need.
—Hebrews 4:16 (KJV)

Jesus gave His life so we might have access to God the Father. When Christ cried out, "It is finished," the promise made to our first parent in Eden was fulfilled. Mercy and grace pour down on all humanity, and because of the Lamb slain from the foundation of the world, we can go boldly to the throne.

Heavenly Father, thank you for being our Father! What a privilege to be called sons and daughters of the most high God! We come boldly to you expecting great things! Knowing who you are and whose we are, why should our hearts be discouraged? No, we are not discouraged because Jesus lives now and forever, amen.

Reflections, Thoughts, and Prayer

_____

_____

_____

_____

_____

_____

July 6

The little foxes ... spoil the vines.
—Song of Solomon 2:15 (KJV)

Deceit, falsehood, and unfaithfulness may be glossed over and hidden from the eyes of man, but not from the eyes of God. The angels of God, who watch the development of character and weigh moral worth, record in the books of heaven these minor transactions which reveal character. (GC 152.4)

Heavenly Father, we thank you for your Holy Spirit, who builds our character. We pray we will cooperate to get rid of the little habits that misrepresent your character from bad eating habits, showing up late, and little white lies to stealing and cheating. Whatever the little habit is, it is keeping us from being our best in you. Help us grow in you we pray in Jesus's name, amen.

Reflections, Thoughts, and Prayer

_____

_____

_____

_____

_____

_____

July 7

The spirit indeed is willing, but the flesh is weak.
—Matthew 26:41 (KJV)

*E*very day is a day to work in overcoming bad habits that displease God. What a work it is to do what is right when we are tempted to do wrong. Individually, we must battle self. We must pray and ask for God's Holy Spirit, we must study and grow in faith and in love, and we must pray as if our lives depended on it. In ourselves, we are no match to conquer self, but when we combine our efforts with divine intervention, victory is ours!

Loving Father, we are a ways off from being what you would have us be, but daily, we surrender to you to work in us to overcome evil habits by the power of your Holy Spirit. Keep us faithful we pray for Christ's sake, amen.

Reflections, Thoughts, and Prayer

_____

_____

_____

_____

_____

_____

July 8

For he that toucheth you toucheth the apple of his eye.
—Zechariah 2:8 (KJV)

*D*o you believe you are precious to our dear Creator? Do you feel your importance in Him? God loved you so much that He sent His only begotten Son to die for you because He knew you were no match to fight the evil one on your own. If you were the only one roaming earth, Jesus would have willingly come to this world riddled with sin and died a cruel and painful death so you might have eternal life. Don't doubt God's love for you. His eyes are upon you every moment. His presence is ever so near.

Heavenly Father, it is reassuring to know that nothing happens to us by accident. Help us trust you always knowing we are the apple of your eye and you care so much for us that you have given everything to see us have eternal life, amen.

Reflections, Thoughts, and Prayer

_____

_____

_____

_____

_____

_____

July 9

I will praise thee; for I am fearfully and wonderfully made.
—Psalm 139:14 (KJV)

When God created everything, He spoke and it was so. But when God made us, He took special care to leave not only His image but also His imprint on our hearts—His Law. It would do us good to take time to know God through His Word and prayer. Take time to praise His holy name.

Heavenly Father, we are able to move, breathe, and function because of your greatness! We have reasons to praise you! Every time we walk, talk, stand, or sit, it is all due to your blessings since the day of creation. We praise you and give you the glory in Jesus's name, amen.

Reflections, Thoughts, and Prayer

_____

_____

_____

_____

_____

_____

_____

July 10

Love must be sincere.
—Romans 12:9 (NIV)

*M*any souls need to be set free from envy, jealousy, backbiting, and evil surmising. It dishonors God when there is discord among His children. We must ask God to remove these terrible weeds growing in our hearts so we can make room for Jesus. When Jesus comes, all darkness is dispelled and love will reign.

Loving Father, search our hearts for anything you disapprove of, bring it to our attention, and remove it. Lord, we desire to be true and sincere Christians. We don't want to be phony or fake. Help us cultivate the habit of being honest and true with you, with ourselves, and with others; we pray this in Jesus's name, amen.

Reflections, Thoughts, and Prayer

_____

_____

_____

_____

_____

_____

_____

July 11

Fight for your brethren, your sons, and your
daughters, your wives, and your houses.
—Nehemiah 4:1 (KJV)

*H*usbands and fathers, you are called to fight for your households. This is spiritual warfare. On your knees, you are more powerful than thousands upon thousands who know not the Lord. You must lead your children to eternal life. Correct their wrongs, control their appetites, and teach them to be obedient to the will of God.

Heavenly Father, we lift up our families to you today. We give you thanks for them. We ask that you put a hedge of protection around them. We ask for husbands everywhere to step up to the plate and be the men you have called them to be and defend their homes on their knees in prayer and fasting because heaven is at stake, amen.

Reflections, Thoughts, and Prayer

_____

_____

_____

_____

_____

_____

_____

July 12

From henceforth now all generations will call me blessed.
—Luke 1:48 (KJV)

If you could see the many blessings God has for you, He would help you surrender your will to His. Isn't it high time you trust God? All who obey Him may be confident that whatever they ask will be granted. Don't doubt or worry when a blessing is delayed. Though it tarries, wait for it. It will surely come.

Heavenly Father, as your children, we are fittingly called blessed by generations! I pray we will be obedient to you so with confidence we may claim the many blessings you have in heaven for those who choose to walk uprightly. May our blessed lives speak volumes for your glory and honor. We pray with thanksgiving in Jesus's name, amen.

Reflections, Thoughts, and Prayer

_____

_____

_____

_____

_____

_____

_____

July 13

Let your light so shine before men, that they may see your
good works, and glorify your Father which is in heaven.
—Matthew 5:16 (KJV)

In all ages God's appointed witnesses have exposed
themselves to reproach and persecution for the truth's
sake. Joseph was maligned and persecuted because he
preserved his virtue and integrity. David, the chosen
messenger of God, was hunted like a beast of prey by
his enemies. Daniel was cast into a den of lions because
he was true to his allegiance to heaven. Job was deprived
of his worldly possessions, and so afflicted in body that
he was abhorred by his relatives, and friends; yet he
maintained his integrity. (AA 575.1)

O my Father, the responsibility to shine is a great one especially
in days of trials and despair. But you wouldn't have called us to
accomplish such a task without equipping us with your Spirit. We trust
you, and by your power, we will shine in Jesus's name, amen.

Reflections, Thoughts, and Prayer

_____

_____

_____

_____

_____

For I know that my redeemer liveth.
—Job 19:25 (KJV)

Job was told by his beloved to curse God and die. But he stayed true to God even though all hope was gone—wealth, health, and children. Job had unwavering faith in God. "The Lord gives, and the Lord takes away. Blessed be the name of the Lord." These words came from a man who had no idea why God had allowed such calamities to come upon him. Because of his faith, Job's last years were his best.

Heavenly Father, I know my Redeemer lives, so no matter where this life may have me, I know like Job, my last years can be my best because Jesus sits at your right hand. Thank you for being Father, who meets all our needs, amen.

Reflections, Thoughts, and Prayer

_____

_____

_____

_____

_____

_____

_____

July 15

Prove me now herewith, saith the LORD of hosts.
—Malachi 3:10 (KJV)

*A*fter you pray according to His Word, believe that God will grant what you have asked and believe His promise. There are times when it is not enough to ask once, so continue to press your petitions with the confidence they will not be denied. Many give up too soon, and many give up very easily; they do not exercise their faith in God. Think how Daniel fasted for three weeks. The answer to Daniel's prayer was stopped short of reaching Daniel because of the enemy's interference. Daniel continued to fast and pray. I shudder to think what would have happened if Daniel hadn't continued to pray.

Loving Father, we welcome the invitation to put you to the test in faith knowing you are more than able and willing to do above and beyond what we expect. Help us not to waver in faith is our prayer, amen.

Reflections, Thoughts, and Prayer

July 16

For this child I prayed; and the LORD hath
given me my petition, which I asked of him.
—1 Samuel 1:27 (KJV)

*P*ray, pray, and pray. Exercise your faith in God, show Him you trust Him, and believe His promises in Jeremiah 29:11. He has great and wonderful thoughts for you. Believe Him. Talk less about your needs and pray more. Recognize God wants to give you the best He has. Tell God what you want in prayer.

Heavenly Father, you want to give us the desires of our hearts, but we hinder you with our lack of faith. Let today be a new beginning when we recommit ourselves to be faithful to you. We will pray until you answer in Jesus's name, amen.

Reflections, Thoughts, and Prayer

_____

_____

_____

_____

_____

_____

_____

July 17

So we fasted and petitioned our God about
this, and he answered our prayer.
—Ezra 8:23 (KJV)

When troubles come your way, look not for help to humanity. Trust everything with God. When we tell others our problems, it makes us weak, and the advice given often makes us even weaker. Trust the divine power of your heavenly Father. He is the Source of all you will ever hope for. The earth is His and everything in it. Go to the unerring, infinite God.

Heavenly Father, we need to follow the examples given to us in the Bible to seek you in our daily living. May we fast and pray until you give us a clear answer. We pray for new habits in prayer for Christ's sake, amen.

Reflections, Thoughts, and Prayer

_____

_____

_____

_____

_____

_____

_____

July 18

> Now unto him that is able to do exceeding
> abundantly above all that we ask or think.
> —Ephesians 3:20 (KJV)

We need less confidence in what we can do and more confidence in what God can do for us. Like the woman with the issue of blood as mentioned in Mark 5:25, we need to reach out to God in faith and touch the hem of His garment. He longs to have us expect great things from Him. Talk faith, walk faith, and live faith. Do not talk defeat or hopelessness into your life, but praise God from whom all blessings flow.

Father, you are good, and you want to give us all that is good. Today, we stand in faith believing for your goodness to take place in our lives so all will see we are indeed children of the most high God. We pray this in the name of Jesus, amen.

Reflections, Thoughts, and Prayer

_____

_____

_____

_____

_____

_____

_____

July 19

I had fainted, unless I had believed to see the
goodness of the LORD in the land of the living.
—Psalm 27:13 (KJV)

*H*ope in God. There is never a time when we may not hope in God. Whatever our necessities, however great our difficulties, and though to all appearance help is impossible, our business is to hope in God, and it will not be in vain. In the Lord's own time, help will come. Believe to see His goodness.

Loving Father, it's clear in your Word that you want to do good things for us right here in the land of the living. You own the world, and you are our Father. We pray for your blessings in health, relationships, finance, and spirituality in the name that is honored, the name of Jesus, amen.

Reflections, Thoughts, and Prayer

July 20

But they that wait upon the LORD shall
renew their strength; They shall mount up
with wings as eagles; they shall run, and not be
weary, and they shall walk, and not faint.
—Isaiah 40:31 (KJV)

*L*earn to wait on God expecting good things, for everything God does is good. Activate that childlike faith. Go to God with your Bible in hand and remind Him of His promises for you to "ask and it shall be given you seek, and ye shall find; knock, and it shall be opened unto you."

Heavenly Father, it is good to wait on you for you are the Giver of life, and all you give is good. We want to soar like eagles and have renewed strength. We are waiting on you. Though at times we are weary, we will continue to pray and seek to know you and desire a deeper walk with you in Jesus's name, amen.

Reflections, Thoughts, and Prayer

_____

_____

_____

_____

_____

_____

July 21

> But my God shall supply all your need according
> to his riches in glory by Christ Jesus.
> —Philippians 4:19 (KJV)

God's riches have no limit. He can give you more than you can ever hope or dream for. All the power that was available to Christ is available to you. The same God is willing; if you ask in faith, you will receive. Persevere like Jacob and do not let go until you are blessed. Be persistent like Elijah and claim all God has for you.

Heavenly Father, we praise you because you are a good and merciful God. We want to claim all you have promised for our lives. We pray you give us strength to stay faithful regardless of our circumstances in Jesus's name, amen.

Reflections, Thoughts, and Prayer

_____

_____

_____

_____

_____

_____

_____

July 22

Hast not thou made an hedge about him, and
about his house, and about all that he hath on every
side? Thou hast blessed the work of his hands,
and his substance is increased in the land.
—Job 1:10 (KJV)

God is in control. Nothing happens without His permission. Wherever you might be right now in life, whatever your situation, trust it all to God. Since the beginning of the world, God has been leading His children. His presence is ever so near. You have His full protecting for He does not sleep or slumber (Psalm 121:3). The enemy knows the power that is fighting for you, but do you know how great is our God? Take time to know the one who has been blessing you time and again.

Heavenly Father, we thank you for the hedge of protection you have placed around us, our loved ones, and all we possess. May we glorify your name with it all in Jesus's name, amen.

Reflections, Thoughts, and Prayer

_____

_____

_____

_____

_____

July 23

And I will make of thee a great nation,
and I will bless thee, and make thy name
great; and thou shalt be a blessing.
—Genesis 12:2 (KJV)

A great deal is said in the Bible about waiting for God. The lesson cannot be too strongly enforced. We easily grow impatient of God's delays. Much of our trouble in life comes out of our restless, sometimes reckless, haste. We cannot wait for the fruit to ripen, but insist on plucking it while it is green. We cannot wait for the answers to our prayers, although the things we ask for may require long years in their preparation for us. We are exhorted to walk with God; but ofttimes God walks very slowly. But there is another phase of the lesson. God often waits for us. (SD 1/26)

*H*eavenly Father, I believe your promises are true. Help me do my part. Help me stay in faith no matter what may be happening around me. Know that as I cooperate with your Holy Spirit, all the blessings will pour in my direction as I run my race leading to the New Jerusalem in Jesus's name, amen.

Reflections, Thoughts, and Prayer

_____

_____

_____

_____

July 24

*Surely goodness and mercy shall follow me
all the days of my life: and I will dwell in
the house of the LORD for ever.*
—Psalm 23:6 (KJV)

"I had never known," said Martin Luther's wife, "what such and such things meant, in such and such psalms, such complaints and workings of spirit; I had never understood the practice of Christian duties, had not God brought me under some affliction."

God's rod is as the schoolmaster's pointer to the child, pointing out the letter, that he may the better take notice of it; thus He points out to us many good lessons we would never otherwise have learned.

Thank you, Father, for your beautiful promise that goodness and mercy are what you want for us. We claim it in Jesus's name, amen.

Reflections, Thoughts, and Prayer

_____

_____

_____

_____

_____

_____

_____

July 25

Every place that the sole of your foot shall tread upon,
that have I given unto you, as I said unto Moses.
—Joshua 1:3 (KJV)

God desires to bless you because you are His child. He desires that all those around you will see the evidence that you are indeed a child of the Living God.

Our hearts should reflect God's character. Our lives should display His love in abundance that even the heathen will know whose we are.

Heavenly Father, we want the world to know we are your children who are called by your name. Help us to humble ourselves before and give us your Spirit; we ask this in Jesus's name, amen.

Reflections, Thoughts, and Prayer

_____

_____

_____

_____

_____

_____

_____

_____

July 26

> There shall not any man be able to stand before thee
> all the days of thy life: as I was with Moses, so I will
> be with thee: I will not fail thee, nor forsake thee.
> —Joshua 1:5 (KJV)

What is thy season this morning? Is it a season of drought? Then that is the season for showers. Is it a season of great heaviness and black clouds? Then that is the season for showers. "As thy day so shall thy strength be." "I will give thee showers of blessing." The word is in the plural. All kinds of blessings God will send. All God's blessings go together, like links in a golden chain. If He gives converting grace, He will also give comforting grace. He will send "showers of blessings." Look up today, O parched plant, and open thy leaves and flowers for a heavenly watering. (C. H. Spurgeon)

We pray Your Holy Spirit will keep us faithful so we may represent you well, amen.

Reflections, Thoughts, and Prayer

_____

_____

_____

_____

_____

July 27

> Only be thou strong and very courageous, that
> thou mayest observe to do according to all the law,
> which Moses my servant commanded thee: turn
> not from it to the right hand or to the left, that
> thou mayest prosper whithersoever thou goest.
> —Joshua 1:7 (KJV)

It is not easy for our Creator to allow trials our way because trials cause great pain. It is equally uneasy for us to go through them, yet we must. It would not help us build character to stay always in one happy and comfortable state. God therefore allows trials. He has given us His Holy Spirit, which gives us strength and courage. Be of good cheer because God is at work.

Heavenly Father, we desire to prosper and have favor from you. Help us seek your ways and walk in your stature. May we obey your laws because the consequences are too great for us. Direct our steps today by the power of your Holy Spirit; we pray this in Jesus's name, amen.

Reflections, Thoughts, and Prayer

_____

_____

_____

_____

_____

_____

July 28

And if a house be divided against itself,
that house cannot stand.
—Mark 3:25 (KJV)

*T*he enemy has come to destroy. He seeks to destroy your home, your faith, your joy, your very soul. Your only safeguard is Jesus. Access through Jesus is through prayer and faith. This is not the time to gain friendship with the world and allow its seductive influence into your heart. This is time to unite in Christ and by His help resist the enemy.

Loving Father, today, I pray for every home and ask your Holy Spirit will put a hedge of protection around them. I pray for peace and unity so the homes will be strengthened and so will our church. May we learn to pray one for another as well as with each other so we may overcome every obstacle in Jesus's name, amen.

Reflections, Thoughts, and Prayer

_____

_____

_____

_____

_____

_____

_____

And God saw their works, that they turned from their
evil way; and God repented of the evil, that he had
said that he would do unto them; and he did it not.
—Jonah 3:10 (KJV)

Some of the storms of life come suddenly: a great
sorrow, a bitter disappointment, a crushing defeat.
Some come slowly. They appear upon the ragged edges
of the horizon no larger than a man's hand, but, trouble
that seems so insignificant spreads until it covers the
sky and overwhelms us. Yet it is in the storm that God
equips us for service. When God wants to make a man
He puts him into some storm. (SD 1/16)

*C*ompassionate God, thank you for your daily mercies. I pray that
as your Holy Spirit works with us and shows us the errors of our
ways, we will do as those in Nineveh did and turn from our evil ways to
receive all the blessings you have in store for us in Jesus's name, amen.

Reflections, Thoughts, and Prayer

_____

_____

_____

_____

_____

_____

July 30

Trust ye not in a friend, put ye not
confidence in a companion.
—Micah 7:5 (KJV)

We know that God is unchanging, yet how many of us lose sight of that as the difficulties of life begin to set in? We forget that what He did one, two, or three thousand years ago He can still do for us today. His divine power to save remains the same; His love for us has not changed.

Take time and confide in Him, and when difficulties arise, never lose sight of the fact He is God.

Heavenly Father, we pray our eyes will be on you only. We want to be among those who cannot be bought by position or status but will stand on your Word and apply it to our daily lives no matter what. Strengthen us by the power of your Holy Spirit; we pray this in Jesus's name, amen.

Reflections, Thoughts, and Prayer

_____

_____

_____

_____

_____

July 31

What time I am afraid, I will trust in thee.
—Psalm 56:3 (KJV)

Luther was once found at a moment of peril and fear, when he had need to grasp unseen strength, sitting in an abstracted mood tracing on the table with his finger the words, "Vivit! vivit!" ("He lives! He lives!"). It is our hope for ourselves, and for His truth, and for humanity. Men come and go; leaders, teachers, thinkers speak and work for a season, and then fall silent and impotent. He abides. They die, but He lives. They are lights kindled, and, therefore, sooner or later quenched; but He is the true light from which they draw all their brightness, and He shines for evermore. (Alexander Maclaren)

*W*e magnify your holy name for the work you are doing in us through your Holy Spirit, developing our characters to have total trust in you, and making us fit for heaven. Continue to guide our every step; that is our humble prayer in Jesus's name, amen.

Reflections, Thoughts, and Prayer

August 1

Is the LORD among us, or not?
—Exodus 17:7 (KJV)

The beginning of anxiety is the end of faith, and the beginning of true faith is the end of anxiety. (George Mueller)

Faith is not a sense, nor sight, nor reason, but a taking God at His Word. (Christmas Evans)

Faithless prayer comes when we ponder the difficulty rather than God's promise. Believe God. Take Him at His word.

Heavenly Father, we are sorry for doubting you and your love for us. We are not different from the children of Israel; nothing is new under the sun. We daily surrender our doubts. Our lives are in your hands, amen.

Reflections, Thoughts, and Prayer

_____

_____

_____

_____

_____

_____

_____

August 2

The LORD is slow to anger, and great in power,
and will not at all acquit the wicked.
—Nahum 1:3 (KJV)

God's character is so pure, so lovely, so holy. He is patient with all, not wanting any to perish but have everlasting life. When hard times come your way, trust in God. If all you remember is that God is still on the throne, that is all you need to trust Him. Believe that He is there working behind the scenes and leading you step by step. Don't run from God to the world seeking ways to ease the pain. He is your almighty friend on whom you can lean.

We are assured by the word of Nahum that you, O God, are good. You break strongholds, and you know those who trust in you. We surrender our lives anew and pray you do not take your Holy Spirit from us. Restore to us the joy of your salvation, and uphold us with your Spirit we pray in Jesus's name, amen.

Reflections, Thoughts, and Prayer

_____

_____

_____

_____

_____

_____

August 3

And whosoever shall compel thee to
go a mile, go with him two.
—Matthew 5:41 (KJV)

*G*od is constantly providing and meeting our needs just in the nick of time. He doesn't open the way in advance of our needs; He doesn't send help before it is needed. The obstacles will be there waiting until we reach them. When we are at the brink of losing it all, God comes to carry the load.

God can use you to be a blessing to others just as others are blessing you. Those in your life right now, take courage with them; God placed them there.

May we cultivate the spirit of excellence going the extra mile to show others that we are a family belonging to one Father, one Creator, one God. We pray for your Holy Spirit to accomplish such a task in us to be more like Jesus every day, amen.

Reflections, Thoughts, and Prayer

_____

_____

_____

_____

_____

O LORD, how long shall I cry, and thou wilt not hear!
even cry out unto thee of violence, and thou wilt not save!
—Habakkuk 1:2 (KJV)

*M*any, like Habakkuk, forget God has a time for everything. They expect the minute they pray, all problems should be solved and difficulties gone. Remember that He is the Potter. He knows how much molding, spinning, and chiseling is needed, and at the right time, voilà!

Heavenly Father, we wait expectantly the second coming of Jesus our Lord and Savior knowing He will come and not tarry. We pray for a fresh anointing of your Holy Spirit today to revive us with energy and holy boldness to give the trumpet that certain sound calling the world to come and worship you, who made heaven and earth and sea and all in them. I pray that like Habakkuk, we may be consistent and persistent never being discouraged even unto death, amen.

Reflections, Thoughts, and Prayer

August 5

Though it tarry, wait for it; because it will surely come.
—Habakkuk 2:3 (KJV)

*D*o you wonder why you are going through such agonizing pain and discomfort? Wait for five to ten years to pass and you will find many others who are experiencing a similar fate. You will tell them how you suffered and how God in His amazing love comforted you. As you are telling the story bringing comfort to other hopeless souls, it will become clear why you had to go down such a path of affliction.

To the true and only wise God we come knowing you haven't given up on us and we must not give up on you. Help us wait in faith expecting great things from you knowing you are able to do it all at the appointed time, amen.

Reflections, Thoughts, and Prayer

_____

_____

_____

_____

_____

_____

_____

August 6

But be gentle unto all men.
—2 Timothy 2:24 (KJV)

*P*aul did not say none of these hurt him. Paul was a tenderhearted soul; he hurt. However, he did not allow circumstances to move him from what he believed was right. His goal was to preach the gospel of Jesus Christ, and nothing was going to shake him, not even death.

We pray for the mastery to attain the fruit of the Holy Spirit. We pray we will not have a form of godliness but allow the inspired Word of the Living God to reprove, rebuke, and exhort with all long-suffering and doctrine. And as we learn from the trials of this life, we will develop the gentle character to deal will others. We pray this in Jesus's name, amen.

Reflections, Thoughts, and Prayer

_____

_____

_____

_____

_____

_____

_____

August 7

> And shall not God avenge his own elect,
> which cry day and night unto him … I tell
> you that he will avenge them speedily.
> —Luke 18:7–8 (KJV)

It takes more courage to walk away from a fight than to actually fight. The season to be still requires an immeasurable amount of strength. Composure is often the highest level of power you can attain. Be still and let God fight for you.

Heavenly Father, we need your Holy Spirit this very hour. Some have been praying and waiting on you for an answer. Give them the courage and patience to stay in faith waiting and expecting something good. At just the right time, we know you will not disappoint because you are God and cannot lie. Every blessing is good for Christ's sake, amen.

Reflections, Thoughts, and Prayer

August 8

By the word of thy lips I have kept me
from the paths of the destroyer.
—Psalm 17:4 (KJV)

By what means did He overcome in the conflict with
Satan? By the word of God. Only by the word could He
resist temptation. "It is written," He said. Every promise
in God's word is ours. When assailed by temptation,
look not to circumstances or to the weakness of self, but
to the power of the word. (DA 123.4)

*H*eavenly Father, may we meditate day and night. Put the beautiful
promises found in your Word in our hearts so when the enemy
comes reminding us of our sins, we too can say, "It is written" and claim
the promise that you love us beyond what we can comprehend. Thank
you for such great love in Jesus's name, amen.

Reflections, Thoughts, and Prayer

_____

_____

_____

_____

_____

_____

August 9

I have overcome the world.
—John 16:33 (KJV)

Life's disappointments are veiled love's appointments.
(Rev. C. A. Fox)

*E*verything that concerns you concerns God. Isaiah 43:4 reminds you that you are precious in His sight. There isn't a thing God hasn't overcome. Go to God and prayer, and He will give you power to stand in His mighty name. Yes, in this world, you will have trouble, but take heart for Christ has overcome the world.

Heavenly Father, may we continue to follow you even when things don't seem to be working in our favor. May we keep to memory that all things work out for good for those who are called by your mighty, holy name, amen.

Reflections, Thoughts, and Prayer

_____

_____

_____

_____

_____

_____

August 10

> And when the woman saw that the tree was good for food,
> and that it was pleasant to the eyes, and a tree to be desired
> to make one wise, she took of the fruit thereof, and did eat,
> and gave also unto her husband with her; and he did eat.
> —Genesis 3:6 (KJV)

Nothing you can do can separate you from the love of God; it says so in Romans 8:35. The moment humanity sinned, the plan of salvation went into full force seeking to reconnect heaven and earth. God gave His all by giving His only Son. Christ gave His all by giving His life. Oh how He loves you and me. Today, we rejoice because we are sons and daughters of the Living God.

Heavenly Father, we pray our appetite will be one that seeks after you day and night. And like Daniel and the Hebrew boys who preferred to perish rather than defile their bodies, we ask for similar appetite control especially these last days. We pray this in Jesus's name, amen.

Reflections, Thoughts, and Prayer

_____

_____

_____

_____

_____

_____

August 11

> Man shall not live by bread alone, but by every
> word that proceedeth out of the mouth of God.
> —Matthew 4:4 (KJV)

*W*hatever you may be going through, your heavenly Father knows about it. A story is told of a professor who asked his deaf and mute students by writing on the board why God had make them this way. One girl got up with tears in her eyes and wrote, "It seemed good in God's sight."

It is encouraging to know that Jesus, our primary example, used the Word to rebuke Satan. Let's stand on the promises of God.

Loving Father, we are thankful for your Word that has brought us great strength in time of need. We pray for temperance in all things especially our appetites so we may regain the mental and moral power to reflect you more and more by the power of your Holy Spirit. We pray this in Jesus's name, amen.

Reflections, Thoughts, and Prayer

_____

_____

_____

_____

_____

_____

August 12

Although the fig tree shall not blossom, neither shall
fruit be in the vines; the labour of the olive shall fail,
and the fields shall yield no meat; Yet I will rejoice in
the LORD, I will joy in the God of my salvation.
—Habakkuk 3:17–18 (KJV)

This life is not free from sorrow and suffering, but rest assured—you
have reason to rejoice. Matthew 10:30 says that every strand of hair
is counted. God is your Provider. There is no need for fear. He will meet
your needs. Just as He cared for Elijah, He will not pass you by.

Lord, I join in the rejoicing because though life's famines are
harassing us, we have this hope and trust in your guidance for Christ's
sake, amen.

Reflections, Thoughts, and Prayer

_____

_____

_____

_____

_____

_____

_____

August 13

For we are labourers together with God.
—1 Corinthians 3:9 (KJV)

*S*peak and act like a laborer of God. Our duty is to let our light shine so all may know the God we serve. Smile, laugh, and be merry for the one you are representing is counting on you to represent Him well.

Thank you for inviting us to labor alongside you, Abba. We pray we will pray one for another. We pray for power from on high. We pray our faith will be genuine. We pray in Jesus's name, amen.

Reflections, Thoughts, and Prayers

_____

_____

_____

_____

_____

_____

_____

_____

_____

August 14

And I heard a voice from heaven saying unto me,
Write, Blessed are the dead which die in the Lord from
henceforth: Yea, saith the Spirit, that they may rest
from their labours; and their works do follow them.
—Revelation 14:13 (KJV)

There is a vast difference between the qualities of old people who have lived flabby, self-indulgent, useless lives and the fiber of those who have sailed all seas and carried all cargoes as the servants of God and the helpers of their fellow men. And when a great and good man sets, the sky of this world is luminous long after he is out of sight. Such a man cannot die out of this world. When he goes he leaves behind him much of himself. (SD 5/31)

*H*eavenly Father, I pray to be a part of your peculiar people not looking to indulge myself but to serve so the impact of my life will resonate with others throughout the ages. That is my humble prayer, amen.

Reflections, Thoughts, and Prayer

_____

_____

_____

_____

_____

August 15

Now therefore thus saith the LORD
of hosts; Consider your ways.
—Haggai 1:5 (KJV)

The Bible tells us that John did no miracles (John 10:41), but John considered his ways. He spoke of Christ and His love for us. He was loyal to the cause of God and bore witness wherever he went. Now, God is asking you to consider your ways. Don't let emotions lead you. Despite your circumstances, shine for Jesus.

Lord, we sow much but reap nothing because we refuse to keep our eyes on you and refuse to humble ourselves and pray for your forgiveness. Renew a right spirit in us and lead us in the path of righteousness so the seeds we sow may fall on good ground and bring about many blessings for your glory. We pray this in Jesus's name, amen.

Reflections, Thoughts, and Prayer

_____

_____

_____

_____

_____

_____

_____

August 16

But the end of all things is at hand: be ye
therefore sober, and watch unto prayer.
—1 Peter 4:7 (KJV)

*S*tudy the prayers of Daniel and learn how he fasted three weeks waiting for an answer. Study the prayers of David and see how God preserved his life time and again. We who are living on the brink of earth's history, let us watch and pray.

Heavenly Father, thank you for the privilege of talking with you each morning for a fresh outpouring of your Holy Spirit so temptation will not catch us unawares. I pray today that the habit to pray as we talk to a friend will begin again for some and begin anew for others. May we look to you with every step we take morning and evening; I pray this in Jesus's name, amen.

Reflections, Thoughts, and Prayer

_____

_____

_____

_____

_____

_____

_____

August 17

And Moses stretched out his hand over the sea; and the
LORD caused the sea to go back by a strong east wind all
that night, and made the sea dry land,
and the waters were divided.
—Exodus 14:21 (KJV)

In this verse there is a comforting message showing how God works in the dark. The real work of God for the children of Israel, was not when they awakened and found that they could get over the Red Sea; but it was "all that night." So there may be a great working in your life when it all seems dark and you cannot see or trace, but yet God is working. (SD 6/04)

Thank you for answered prayer when we pray, and thank you for the blessings even when we forget to pray or are too discouraged to pray. Thank you for being faithful, amen.

Reflections, Thoughts, and Prayer

_____

_____

_____

_____

_____

_____

_____

August 18

For he that toucheth you toucheth the apple of his eye.
—Zechariah 2:8 (KJV)

God is in control. If you have surrendered to Him, the enemy of souls has no power over you. He is limited by the blood of Jesus. Wherever you are right now, however big the boulder might appear, remember that God has placed you there. You are the apple of His eye; no one can touch you without permission (Job 1:12).

Heavenly Father, thank you for calling us out of the world and making us the apple of your eye. Help us remember as we face difficulties and ominous circumstances that it is not by might or by power but by your Holy Spirit that we can overcome in Jesus's name, amen.

Reflections, Thoughts, and Prayer

_____

_____

_____

_____

_____

_____

_____

_____

August 19

These are the things that ye shall do; Speak ye
every man the truth to his neighbour; execute the
judgment of truth and peace in your gates.
—Zechariah 8:16 (KJV)

*W*e need the fresh anointing of God's Holy Spirit every day. It would be unwise to seek to complete our daily task without proper nutrition, so it is unwise to seek to deal with others without eating the heavenly manna.

To speak peace, you must have peace; to speak truth, you must have truth. Daily seek Him in His Word for newness of life.

Clean our hearts, Lord, so whatever is offensive to you will be offensive to us. The time has come when the habits that hinder our relationship with you and prevent others from seeing our light be put away. We ask this in Jesus's name, amen.

Reflections, Thoughts, and Prayer

_____

_____

_____

_____

_____

_____

_____

August 20

Turn you to the strong hold, ye prisoners of hope: even
to day do I declare that I will render double unto thee.
—Zechariah 9:12 (KJV)

There is never a time when we cannot hope in God. At all times, in
all places, in all sufferings, and in all pains, at the darkest hour of
the night or in the depth of the valley, hope in the Lord your God, the
Source of all things. His resources are limitless. He has a thousand ways
to meet your needs though you know nothing about them. It is good to
hope in God. Hope thou in the Lord!

May each one of us who professes to be your children and follower
of the lovely Jesus remain steadfast in keeping the Commandments,
meditate on your Word, and draw closer to you each day in prayer
claiming the promises in Jesus's name, amen.

Reflections, Thoughts, and Prayer

_____

_____

_____

_____

_____

_____

August 21

And she shall bring forth a son, and thou shalt call his
name JESUS: for he shall save his people from their sins.
—Matthew 1:21 (KJV)

The promise of Jesus's birth was made to our first parents in the garden of Eden soon after they sinned (Genesis 3:15). In the fullness of time, Christ was born. Christ identifies Himself with us. He understands our sorrows and temptations. He knows what we need. Waiting and expecting great things from God sometimes means we must wait to the very last hour.

Heavenly Father, thank you for loving us so much that you sent your only Son to save us from eternal death. No one else could have saved us except for Emmanuel, God with us. He taught us how to love, give, and respect one another, and He redeemed us by the blood that flowed from His body so we may live more abundantly. We have reasons to praise your holy name, amen, amen, and amen.

Reflections, Thoughts, and Prayer

_____

_____

_____

_____

_____

_____

August 22

> For verily I say unto you, Till heaven and
> earth pass, one jot or one tittle shall in no wise
> pass from the law, till all be fulfilled.
> —Matthew 5:18 (KJV)

Jesus came to fulfill the law. He is also fulfilling something in you this moment. Jesus is teaching you to trust Him. He wants you to come to Him first with everything. Unclench your heart, surrender to Him, and receive His blessing of life eternal.

Deception is rampant these last days. We thank you, heavenly Father, for the Word and the examples of Christ left for us to follow. May we learn to meditate on your holy Word, allowing the Holy Spirit to be our guide and Comforter along the way; we ask this in Jesus's name, amen.

Reflections, Thoughts, and Prayer

_____

_____

_____

_____

_____

_____

_____

August 23

> But thou, when thou prayest, enter into thy closet,
> and when thou hast shut thy door, pray to thy
> Father which is in secret; and thy Father which
> seeth in secret shall reward thee openly.
> —Matthew 6:6 (KJV)

Prayer is the opening of the heart to God as to a friend. Not that it is necessary in order to make known to God what we are, but in order to enable us to receive Him. Prayer does not bring God down to us, but brings us up to Him. (CSA 26.3)

*H*eavenly Father, thank you for pointing to us the habits we are to cultivate in prayer. Help us come before you with humble and contrite hearts. Help us be careful of our motives when we pray. Our desire is to do your will in thought, word, and deed. Give us what we lack by the power of your Holy Spirit, amen.

Reflections, Thoughts, and Prayer

_____

_____

_____

_____

_____

_____

August 24

He that hath no rule over his own spirit is like a
city that is broken down, and without walls.
—Proverbs 25:28 (KJV)

Trials do not last forever; they come and go. When trials come, remember they are coming from your heavenly Father. Do not complain or murmur wondering when they will end. Instead, teach your spirit to praise God through it all. If God allows affliction to come your way, after it has served its purpose, God will remove it. Be still and know that He is God.

Loving Father, we praise you today for your love and protection throughout our existence. We pray that by the power of your Holy Spirit, we will take control of ourselves and choose to be joyful in spite of our issues. All the weight of the world we turn over to you. We are setting our minds for a great day because this is the day the Lord has made, and we'll be glad in it, amen.

Reflections, Thoughts, and Prayer

_____

_____

_____

_____

_____

August 25

Who against hope believed in hope,
that he might become the father of many nations,
according to that which was spoken.
—Romans 4:18 (KJV)

We shall never forget a remark that George Mueller once made to a gentleman who had asked him the best way to have strong faith. "The only way," replied the patriarch of faith, "to learn strong faith is to endure great trials. I have learned my faith by standing firm amid severe testings." This is very true. The time to trust is when all else fails. (SD 6/2)

*H*eavenly Father, we ask to trust you, but when the trials come, we ask why. Help us believe in you and fully trust your leading knowing it will all work out, amen.

Reflections, Thoughts, and Prayer

_____

_____

_____

_____

_____

_____

August 26

Moreover if thy brother shall trespass against thee,
go and tell him his fault between thee and him alone:
if he shall hear thee, thou hast gained thy brother.
—Matthew 18:15 (KJV)

The power of evil triumphs when brothers and sisters are at war with one another. An even bigger dishonor to God is when they choose to settle the matter in the courts. Stop and think of His great mercy toward you. Does your brother not deserve the same treatment from you? Does your sister not deserve the same grace you have received freely from above? Tell your neighbors how you feel, and leave the rest with God.

Heavenly Father, may we put these words of wisdom into application in our lives so we may not put you to shame. May we be like the meek and lowly Jesus and settle our differences with one another; we pray this in Jesus's name, amen.

Reflections, Thoughts, and Prayer

_____

_____

_____

_____

_____

_____

August 27

> Now no chastening for the present seemeth to
> be joyous, but grievous: nevertheless afterward
> it yieldeth the peaceable fruit of righteousness
> unto them which are exercised thereby.
> —Hebrews 12:11 (KJV)

If God had told Abraham in Haran that he must wait for thirty years until he pressed the promised child to his bosom, his heart would have failed him. So, in gracious love, the length of the weary years was hidden. The set time came at last; and then the laughter that filled the patriarch's home made the aged pair forget the long and weary vigil. Take heart, waiting one, thou waitest for One who cannot disappoint thee; and who will not be five minutes behind the appointed moment. (SD 5/24)

Heavenly Father, at times in life, we don't like where we are, but still, we trust. We know you are working being the scenes of our lives to give us a great finish, amen.

Reflections, Thoughts, and Prayer

August 28

Wherefore glorify ye the LORD in the fires.
—Isaiah 24:15 (KJV)

The man whose faith has been deeply tested and who has come off victorious is the man to whom supreme tests must come. The finest jewels are most carefully cut and polished; the hottest fires try the most precious metal. Abraham would never have been called the Father of the Faithful if he had not been proved to the uttermost. "Take thy son, thine only son, whom thou lovest." See him going with a chastened, wistful, yet humbly obedient heart up Moriah's height, with the idol of his heart beside him about to be sacrificed at the command of God whom he had faithfully loved and served! (SD 5/9)

*M*ay we give you our idols when you ask us for them and still keep a cheerful, trusting ear toward you we pray in Jesus's name, amen.

Reflections, Thoughts, and Prayer

_____

_____

_____

_____

_____

_____

August 29

Be ye glad and rejoice for ever in that which I create.
—Isaiah 65:18 (KJV)

A king went into his garden one morning and found everything withered and dying. He asked the oak what the trouble was. He found it was sick of life and determined to die because it was not tall and beautiful like the pine. The pine was all out of heart because it could not bear grapes like the vine, and so on all through the garden. Coming to a heart's-ease, he found its bright face lifted as cheery as ever. "Well, heart's-ease, You do not seem to be the least disheartened." "No, I am not. I thought that if you wanted an oak, or a pine, or a lilac, you would have planted one; but as I knew you wanted a heart's-ease, I am determined to be the best little heart's-ease I can."

May we keep a cheerful countenance in your presence always and enjoy where we are in our lives as we walk with you, amen.

Reflections, Thoughts, and Prayer

_____

_____

_____

_____

_____

_____

August 30

The prayer of faith shall save the sick, and
the Lord shall raise him up; and if he have
committed sins, they shall be forgiven him.
—James 5:15 (KJV)

God desires for our faith to be pure and active. Pure because we believe what He says. Active because we receive and thank Him for answering even before we see the blessing. Oh my dear friend, believe in God.

And so today, we wonder no more. We need to increase the compassion we have one for another and show deep love through our actions one for another. Help us implement the recipe you have given us in Isaiah 58 so when we pray, our prayers will be heard and answered. Give us your Holy Spirit in Jesus's name, amen.

Reflections, Thoughts, and Prayer

_____

_____

_____

_____

_____

_____

_____

August 31

And Jesus said unto the centurion, Go thy way; and
as thou hast believed, so be it done unto thee. And
his servant was healed in the selfsame hour.
—Matthew 8:13, 20 (KJV)

*B*lessed are they that have not seen and yet have believed (John 20:29). The centurion had such a faith. He knew the power Jesus possessed. He knew that if Jesus spoke healing, his servant would be healed. Jesus was amazed that in all Israel, only one had so great a faith. God is able to speak great things into your life if you simply believe.

Thank you, Lord, for your lesson on faith. Your Word said if we have the faith as small as a mustard seed, we could move mountains. We pray for power so when we pray, things will happen in Jesus's name, amen.

Reflections, Thoughts, and Prayer

_____

_____

_____

_____

_____

_____

_____

September 1

> And when he was come into the house, the blind men
> came to him: and Jesus saith unto them, Believe ye that
> I am able to do this? They said unto him, Yea, Lord.
> —Matthew 9:28 (KJV)

The same Jesus who made the blind to see is with you through all the changes of life. There is never a need to fear when Jesus is so near. Because He lives, you can look forward to your tomorrow.

Thank you, Lord, for the measure of faith you have given us. May we like the blind man exercise it so you may supply all our needs and embolden us to tell of your goodness in the land of the living even today. We pray in the most powerful name in the universe, the name of Jesus, amen.

Reflections, Thoughts, and Prayer

_____

_____

_____

_____

_____

_____

_____

September 2

At that time Jesus answered and said, I thank thee, O
Father, Lord of heaven and earth, because thou hast hid
these things from the wise and prudent, and hast revealed
them unto babes. Even so, Father: for so it seemed good
in thy sight. All things are delivered unto me of my
Father: and no man knoweth the Son, but the Father.
—Matthew 11:25–27 (KJV)

God is so beautiful in His dealing with us. He reveals to us little by little as we need to know. He doesn't show us the whole picture all at once because He doesn't want to overwhelm us. Instead, bit by bit at just the right moment, He imparts knowledge for the season we are in. He promises to be with us even unto death. It is good to know that the Lord is my Shepherd and I shall not want for anything.

Thank you, Lord, for your many examples of prayer. Continue to teach us the lifestyle that leads to a powerful Christian walk with you; we pray this in Jesus's name, amen.

Reflections, Thoughts, and Prayer

_____

_____

_____

_____

_____

September 3

Behold, I send you forth as sheep in the midst of wolves:
be ye therefore wise as serpents, and harmless as doves.
—Matthew 10:16 (KJV)

A s sheep, we are in need of a shepherd. Jesus is the Good Shepherd who accompanies us wherever life takes us. By His Holy Spirit, He is with us always. Daily, we should lean on Christ to show us the way. Daily, we should ask God how we might live among the wolves. We should pray for wisdom that He will freely give anyone who asks. We should pray for gentleness so we may reach others for His kingdom.

Father, thank you for being a God of order. As our Pattern, you taught us to start our witnessing at home and in our churches because it is there we receive the honing and shaping to meet the wolves in sheep's clothing. It is there we learn to become true missionaries for you. Give us the wisdom from above we pray in Jesus's name, amen.

Reflections, Thoughts, and Prayers

_____

_____

_____

_____

_____

_____

_____

September 4

I will arise and go to my father, and will say unto him,
Father, I have sinned against heaven, and before thee.
—Luke 15:18 (KJV)

I should expect life in a dead man as spiritual life in a
prayerless soul! Our spirituality and our fruitfulness are
always in proportion to the reality of our prayers. If,
then, we have at all wandered away from home in the
matter of prayer, let us today resolve. (KC 59)

*H*eavenly Father, thank you for always looking out for us and for our
good. Though we are prone to wander from you, your door remains
open for us to come back and ask for your forgiveness and blessing. There
in your presence we come to realize you have never left our side because
of your great love. We thank you today in Jesus's name, amen.

Reflections, Thoughts, and Prayer

_____

_____

_____

_____

_____

_____

_____

September 5

> For if ye forgive men their trespasses, your
> heavenly Father will also forgive you.
> —Matthew 6:14 (KJV)

We are not forgiven because we forgive, but as we forgive. The ground of all forgiveness is found in the unmerited love of God, but by our attitude toward others we show whether we have made that love our own. Wherefore Christ says, "With what judgment ye judge, ye shall be judged; and with what measure ye mete, it shall be measured to you again." (COL 251.4)

Thank you, Father, for teaching us to avoid concentrating on others' trespasses while expecting our trespasses to be forgiven. That we like you be loving and kind and inspired by your Holy Spirit we pray in Jesus's name, amen.

Reflections, Thoughts, and Prayer

_____

_____

_____

_____

_____

_____

September 6

I will not let thee go, except thou bless
me ... And he blessed him there.
—Genesis 32:26, 29 (KJV)

Jacob got the victory and the blessing not by wrestling, but by clinging. His limb was out of joint and he could struggle no longer, but he would not let go. Unable to wrestle, he wound his arms around the neck of his mysterious antagonist and hung all his helpless weight upon him, until at last he conquered. We will not get victory in prayer until we too cease our struggling, giving up our own will and throw our arms about our Father's neck in clinging faith. (S/D 5/28)

*H*eavenly Father, we pray today for a special blessing we seek. We have prayed day after day and will continue to pray with unwavering faith until we see the prayer is answered. You are the Source of our existence, and like Jacob, we will not let you go until you bless us, amen.

Reflections, Thoughts, and Prayer

_____

_____

_____

_____

_____

September 7

He said, Bring them hither to me.
—Matthew 14:18 (KJV)

Are you encompassed with needs at this very moment, and almost overwhelmed with difficulties, trials, and emergencies? These are all divinely provided vessels for the Holy Spirit to fill, and if you but rightly understood their meaning, they would become opportunities for receiving new blessings. Bring these vessels to God. Hold them steadily before Him in faith and prayer. Keep still, and stop your own restless working until He begins to work. Give Him a chance to work, and He will surely do so; and the very trials that threatened to overcome you with discouragement and disaster, will become God's opportunity for the revelation of His grace and glory in your life, as you have never known Him before. "Bring them (all needs) to me." (A. B. Simpson SD)

Heavenly Father, we bring all our wounded hearts, shattered dreams, and broken toys to you. We pray for faith and to see our sorrows turn to joy, amen.

Reflections, Thoughts, and Prayer

_____

_____

_____

_____

September 8

> Now no chastening for the present seemeth to
> be joyous, but grievous: nevertheless afterward
> it yieldeth the peaceable fruit of righteousness
> unto them which are exercised thereby.
> —Hebrews 12:11 (KJV)

If God had told Abraham in Haran that he must wait for thirty years until he pressed the promised child to his bosom, his heart would have failed him. So, in gracious love, the length of the weary years was hidden. The set time came at last; and then the laughter that filled the patriarch's home made the aged pair forget the long and weary vigil. Take heart, waiting one, thou waitest for One who cannot disappoint thee; and who will not be five minutes behind the appointed moment. (SD 5/24)

Heavenly Father, there are times in life when we don't like where we are, but we still trust you are working being the scenes of our lives to give us a great finish, amen.

Reflections, Thoughts, and Prayer

September 9

My brethren, count it all joy when
ye fall into divers temptations.
—James 1:2 (KJV)

If Job could have known as he sat there in the ashes, bruising his heart on this problem of Providence-that in the trouble that had come upon him he was doing what one man may do to work out the problem for the world, he might again have taken courage. No man lives to himself. Job's life is but your life and mine written in larger text. So, then, though we may not know what trials wait on any of us, we can believe that as the days in which Job wrestled with his dark maladies are the only days that make him worth remembrance, and but for which his name had never been written in the book of life, so the days through which we struggle, finding no way, but never losing the light, will be the most significant we are called to live. (Robert Collyer)

*H*eavenly Father, give us your Holy Spirit to endure our trials because we never know who is watching and waiting for us to run away from it all. Keep us faithful we pray, amen.

Reflections, Thoughts, and Prayer

_____

_____

_____

_____

September 10

And lead us not into temptation, but deliver us from evil.
—Matthew 6:13 (KJV)

God doesn't tempt us. When faced with temptations, walk away. Do not encourage it. Pray for deliverance. Talk to God, and He will provide an escape. When you play with temptations, you place yourself in the enemy's territory. God wants to deliver you.

Loving Father who art in heaven, we are thankful that you do not lead us to temptation. Thank you for showing us a better way—Jesus. We want to live victorious lives. Help us live pure and holy lives that are pleasing to you. Thank you for delivering us from the evil one and giving us full, abundant lives, amen.

Reflections, Thoughts, and Prayer

_____

_____

_____

_____

_____

_____

_____

September 11

Not that I speak in respect of want: for I have learned,
in whatsoever state I am, therewith to be content.
—Philippians 4:11 (KJV)

God specializes in the impossible. When life gets the most difficult, that is when God reveals to us what He can do. He bids us to trust and obey. If we trust Him, we can be content in whatever situation we find ourselves. God has placed you there for a purpose. Glorify Him.

Heavenly Father, today, we pray for a similar experience where we can be content no matter what. Your thoughts toward us are good thoughts, and we want to glorify your name by trusting your leading even when we are in the slumps. Give us an attitude like Paul we pray, amen.

Reflections, Thoughts, and Prayer

_____

_____

_____

_____

_____

_____

_____

September 12

Jesus saith unto him, I am the way, the truth, and the
life: no man cometh unto the Father, but by me.
—John 14:6 (KJV)

*D*on't let discouragement cause you not to point others to Christ.
Your attitude plays a major role in exalting the Savior of the world
to others. More people are longing to find the way that leads to Jesus,
in whom we have eternal life. Be fortified in the Word. Represent your
Creator well.

Heavenly Father, today, we pray the way we live our lives will preach
the biggest sermon of love that will lead many to your kingdom. Help us
accept the gift of eternal life given to all who call on the name of your
Son, Jesus, who is our all and all, amen.

Reflections, Thoughts, and Prayer

_____

_____

_____

_____

_____

_____

_____

September 13

Cast me not away from thy presence;
and take not thy holy spirit from me.
—Psalm 51:11 (KJV)

*W*e need God's Holy Spirit to guide us morning, noon, and night. Pray daily for His Spirit and amid the storms of life; your joy shall remain steadfast, and your cup shall overflow with blessings from above.

Heavenly Father, today, we pray for the outpouring of your Holy Spirit. We need the latter rain to fall upon us. These last days' error is mingled with truth, and many are being led down the road to perdition. Give us your Spirit so we may study and know the truth for ourselves. We want to enter the straight and narrow path that leads to eternal life, amen.

Reflections, Thoughts, and Prayer

_____

_____

_____

_____

_____

_____

_____

September 14

Behold, I see the heavens opened, and the Son
of man standing on the right hand of God.
—Acts 7:56 (KJV)

When Stephen was being stoned, he looked to Jesus and saw Him standing next to His Father. Stephen knew God was with him watching it all. Today, I urge you to cling to Jesus even in the most ominous times.

Heavenly Father, today, we look to you for our hope. Like Stephen as he was being stoned saw Christ sitting at your right hand, may we look to you and see you have never left or forsaken us no matter what we may be going through, amen.

Reflections, Thoughts, and Prayer

_____

_____

_____

_____

_____

_____

_____

_____

September 15

I am he that liveth, and was dead; and, behold, I am alive
for evermore, Amen; and have the keys of
hell and of death.
—Revelation 1:18 (KJV)

There is no place for despondency when you are serving the Author and Finisher of your faith. Jesus is alive. In Him is your hope of life eternal. He has great plans for your life. In Jeremiah 29:11, He reminds you of the thoughts He has toward you to give you a life of peace. Worry about nothing for Jesus is alive!

Glory to God on high! Father, we thank you that through the blood of the Lamb, we are free. We thank you that the enemy cannot hold the dead in his grasp because Jesus has the keys of death. Today, we rejoice because we know that though we should die, we live when we die in Christ. Hallelujah forever, amen.

Reflections, Thoughts, and Prayer

September 16

I shall not be moved.
—Psalm 10:6 (KJV)

You have made your request of God, but the answer does not come. What are you to do? Keep on believing God's Word; never be moved away from it by what you see or feel, and thus as you stand steady, enlarged power and experience is being developed. The fact of looking at the apparent contradiction as to God's Word and being unmoved from your position of faith make you stronger on every other line. Often God delays purposely, and the delay is just as much an answer to your prayer as is the fulfillment when it comes. (SD 5/12)

*H*eavenly Father, you are the Captain of our lives. And as long as we stay under your command, we will reach our destination victoriously overcoming every obstacle along the way. May we remain planted firmly in your Word; that is our prayer in Jesus's name, amen.

Reflections, Thoughts, and Prayer

_____

_____

_____

_____

_____

_____

September 17

And the LORD said, I have surely seen
the affliction of my people.
—Exodus 3:7 (KJV)

When first affliction comes upon us, how everything
gives way! Our clinging, tendril hopes are snapped, and
our heart lies prostrate like a vine that the storm has
torn from is trellis; but when the first shock is past, and
we are able to look up, and say, "It is the Lord," faith lifts
the shattered hopes once more, and binds them fast to
the feet of God. Thus the end is confidence, safety, and
peace. (Selected SD)

*H*eavenly Father, we are grateful that you are familiar with every
detail of our lives, even our afflictions and trials. Thank you for
keeping a watchful eye on us and making a way for us when we are not
able to see a way, amen.

Reflections, Thoughts, and Prayer

_____

_____

_____

_____

_____

September 18

Or what man is there of you, whom if his son ask
bread, will he give him a stone? Or if he ask a fish,
will he give him a serpent? If ye then, being evil,
know how to give good gifts unto your children,
how much more shall your Father which is in
heaven give good things to them that ask him?
—Matthew 7:9–11 (KJV)

I saw that the servants of God and the church were too
easily discouraged. When they asked their Father in
heaven for things which they thought they needed, and
these did not immediately come, their faith wavered,
their courage fled, and a murmuring feeling took
possession of them. This, I saw, displeased God. (GW92
112.1)

Thank you, Father, for loving us with an everlasting love. Thank
you for reassuring us throughout your Word that you have good
plans for us. May we meditate on all your goodness. Take away our
disappointments we ask, amen.

Reflections, Thoughts, and Prayer

_____

_____

_____

_____

_____

September 19

And Esau came from the field, and he was faint.
—Genesis 25:29 (KJV)

*W*hen you feel faint, weary, and tired of all the trials this world can bring, God knows your battle; He knows the warrior is a child. This is the time to rest in God. Stay quiet because you don't want past blessings to become insignificant. Stay in prayer, and God will give you the strength to take one step forward and then another. Esau saw only his current condition and lost greatly his blessing. Let's learn how to surrender our needs to God and allow Him to fight for us.

Heavenly Father, when the trials are too hard to bear, we lean on you to see us through. Thank you for sending the right people into our lives to say the right things at just the right time. We pray for your peace in Jesus's name, amen.

Reflections, Thoughts, and Prayer

_____

_____

_____

_____

_____

_____

September 20

> But the fruit of the Spirit is love, joy, peace,
> longsuffering, gentleness, goodness, faith.
> —Galatians 5:22 (KJV)

*G*row in grace. Yield to God's Holy Spirit, and allow the fruit of His Spirit to grow in you. He is the Gardener of your character who allows just the right trials to come your way so the trimming and pruning can take place. When He is finished, your image will be restored to one of love, joy, peace, long-suffering, gentleness, goodness, and faith.

Heavenly Father, we need and desire clean hearts that will reflect Christ. We need tenderness, compassion, and love to ooze from our spirits. Open our eyes so we can see as heaven sees; we pray this in Jesus's name, amen.

Reflections, Thoughts, and Prayer

_____

_____

_____

_____

_____

_____

_____

September 21

And I set my face unto the Lord God, to seek by prayer
and supplications, with fasting, and sackcloth, and ashes.
—Daniel 9:3 (KJV)

Perseverance is one major element needed when we pray, and faith is the other. Daniel persevered in prayer with fasting, sackcloth, and ashes. He needed power that could come only from the throne of God. He needed an answer. We are told how the enemy was holding his blessing back. What would have become of that blessing if Daniel had not persevered? Let us make it a habit to seek God in prayer and take time to fast with sackcloth and ashes because we do not know what is going on behind the scenes of this spiritual warfare.

Heavenly Father, today, we continue to plead and intercede for one another. We pray we will be victorious and live lives of prayer. May we persevere in prayer like those who are mentioned in biblical times. Help us follow their example and never give up until what we are praying for is given a clear answer from you we pray, amen.

Reflections, Thoughts, and Prayer

_____

_____

_____

_____

_____

_____

September 22

Enter ye in at the strait gate: for wide is the gate,
and broad is the way, that leadeth to destruction,
and many there be which go in thereat.
—Matthew 7:13 (KJV)

These roads are distinct, separate, in opposite directions. One leads to eternal life, the other to eternal death. I saw the distinction between these roads, also the distinction between the companies traveling them. The roads are opposite; one is broad and smooth, the other narrow and rugged. So the parties that travel them are opposite in character, in life, in dress, and in conversation. (CET 156.1)

Thank you, Lord, for this message and the invitation to stay in the path of righteousness as we enter the straight gate. Help us as your children to unite with each other in love and encourage one another praising you all the way, amen.

Reflections, Thoughts, and Prayer

_____

_____

_____

_____

_____

_____

September 23

When the enemy shall come in like a flood, the Spirit
of the LORD shall lift up a standard against him.
—Isaiah 59:19 (KJV)

*W*hen hardships perplex you on every side, call on God and He will answer. God has seen you through difficult times, and He can see you through this. Do not allow your faith to grow dim, but look to the past and see how He has led you. Praise Him even now because you know He'll do it again. Keep your joy and peace because God is fighting for you.

Heavenly Father, today, we praise you for the wonderful work you are doing in us. We pray our faith in you will get stronger especially during the times of tribulation knowing you have the power to stop the enemy in his tracks, amen.

Reflections, Thoughts, and Prayer

_____

_____

_____

_____

_____

_____

_____

September 24

I have chosen thee in the furnace of affliction.
—Isaiah 48:10 (KJV)

The furnace is to polish you and see that you are wholly dependent on God. This is a time for your faith to be strengthened. Little trials should not cause your faith to waver. Bit by bit, your experiences with God should increase your faith. Remember that the Lord gives you strength to face every new challenge and trial. He gives you strength to go on. He gives you strength to go up. Yes, my friend, the furnace fires are not sent to destroy but to sanctify.

The afflictions of life are not easy, but I'm thankful to have a friend in Jesus who understands the trials we must endure because He was tested on all points and did not succumb to sin. Keep us faithful we pray, amen.

Reflections, Thoughts, and Prayer

_____

_____

_____

_____

_____

_____

September 25

> The LORD is good; his mercy is everlasting;
> and his truth endureth to all generations.
> —Psalm 100:5 (KJV)

Our Lord and Saviour laid aside His dominion, His riches and glory, and sought after us, that He might save us from misery and make us like Himself. He humbled Himself and took our nature that we might be able to learn of Him and, imitating His life of benevolence and self-denial, follow Him step by step to heaven. You cannot equal the copy; but you can resemble it and, according to your ability, do likewise. (2T 169.4)

*W*e have seen your faithfulness over and over; from generation to generation, you have been faithful. Today, I pray we will focus on your goodness and the plan of salvation established even before sin entered our world so we might have eternal life, amen.

Reflections, Thoughts, and Prayer

_____

_____

_____

_____

_____

September 26

Greater love hath no man than this, that a
man lay down his life for his friends.
—John 15:13 (KJV)

Jesus laid down His life to save us from eternal damnation. What love is this? Love so unconditional, so limitless. That is the love we need to demonstrate. A love that bears all things, believes all things, hopes for the best in all things, and endures all things. There's no greater love than this.

Heavenly Father, words are not enough to express my gratitude for your great sacrifice on Calvary when Christ died for all humanity. That we not put your love to shame by our actions or complaints and that we follow the example of Jesus by the power of your Holy Spirit we pray in Jesus's name, amen.

Reflections, Thoughts, and Prayer

_____

_____

_____

_____

_____

_____

_____

But the very hairs of your head are all numbered.
—Matthew 10:30 (KJV)

*H*ow precious you are to the King of the universe. Jesus laid down all His riches and power because you were in need of a Savior. He humbled Himself, was spat on, rejected, abused, and nailed to a tree on Calvary. But what crushed Him was the sins He carried. He did all this to show you just how much He loves you and just how much He yearns to be near you. He knows you very well. Won't you take time to know Him? Oh how He loves you!

Loving Father, what a wonderful example of your love that you know how may hairs we have on our heads. We want closeness with you. Help us seek you daily taking time to be intimate with you. We pray this in Jesus's name, amen.

Reflections, Thoughts, and Prayer

_____

_____

_____

_____

_____

_____

September 28

He said, bring them hither to me.
—Matthew 14:18 (KJV)

Are you encompassed with needs at this very moment, and almost overwhelmed with difficulties, trials, and emergencies? These are all divinely provided vessels for the Holy Spirit to fill, and if you but rightly understood their meaning, they would become opportunities for receiving new blessings. Bring these vessels to God. Hold them steadily before Him in faith and prayer. Keep still, and stop your own restless working until He begins to work. Give Him a chance to work, and He will surely do so; and the very trials that threatened to overcome you with discouragement and disaster, will become God's opportunity for the revelation of His grace and glory in your life, as you have never known Him before. "Bring them (all needs) to me." (A. B. Simpson SD)

Heavenly Father, we bring all our wounded hearts, shattered dreams, and broken toys to you. We pray for faith and see our sorrows turn to joy, amen.

Reflections, Thoughts, and Prayer

_____

_____

_____

_____

September 29

And Enoch walked with God.
—Genesis 5:22 (KJV)

*O*ne of my favorite hymns starts with, "I come to the garden alone while the dew is still on the roses" and God walks and talks with me, and He tells me I am His own. How peaceful it is to walk with God. No matter what is happening around you, tranquility is yours when you walk with God; serenity is yours when you walk with God. When He reassures you of whose you are, you have strength for your days of affliction.

What an honor it is to walk with you, eternal Father. We ask that we cultivate the habit of praying morning, noon, and night. Help us allow your Holy Spirit to complete the work in us. We pray that one day it may be said of us that we walked with you. We pray in Jesus's name, amen.

Reflections, Thoughts, and Prayer

_____

_____

_____

_____

_____

_____

September 30

If thou faint in the day of adversity, thy strength is small.
—Proverbs 24:10 (KJV)

The man who forms the habit of beginning without finishing has simply formed the habit of failure. The man who begins to pray about a thing and does not pray it through to a successful issue of answer has formed the same habit in prayer. To faint is to fail; then defeat begets disheartenment, and unfaith in the reality of prayer, which is fatal to all success. But someone says, "How long shall we pray? Do we not come to a place where we may cease from our petitions and rest the matter in God's hands?" There is but one answer. Pray until the thing you are praying for has actually been granted, or until you have the assurance in your heart that it will be. (The Practice of Prayer)

*H*eavenly Father, we need to learn how to persevere in prayer. Please teach us to pray as John taught his disciples, amen.

Reflections, Thoughts, and Prayer

_____

_____

_____

_____

_____

October 1

For ye are dead, and your life is hid with Christ in God.
—Colossians 3:3 (KJV)

*I*s it possible to come to a place where nothing can upset us or disturb our peace? Yes. We need to surrender our wills to God. To be hid in Christ means that Christ is doing the talking, walking, and fighting for us. Paul came to a place where he considered all things a joy. We can too.

Loving Father, we thank you for the sacrifice of your only Son wherein we have nothing to fear, not even death. We pray your Holy Spirit will ever be with us guiding our every step. Even when we find ourselves in the shadow of the valley of death, may we fear no evil knowing you are with us, amen.

Reflections, Thoughts, and Prayer

_____

_____

_____

_____

_____

_____

_____

_____

October 2

> Know ye not, that to whom ye yield yourselves servants
> to obey, his servants ye are to whom ye obey; whether
> of sin unto death, or of obedience unto righteousness?
> —Romans 6:16 (KJV)

It would be wise to yield to the God of all created things. When you yield to God, your peace remains undisturbed to face the little nuances as well as great and heavy trials. The joy of the Lord shall be yours. When we yield to temptation, we walk down a path that eventually leads to destruction.

Heavenly Father, we desire to place ourselves on the path that leads to everlasting life. Help us put away cherished sins and not enter temptation. Thank you for assuring us that you have made a way of escape if we should find ourselves in limbo. That we may we move cautiously with your Holy Spirit is our plea in Jesus's name, amen.

Reflections, Thoughts, and Prayer

_____

_____

_____

_____

_____

_____

_____

October 3

And he said, Oh let not the Lord be angry, and I will
speak yet but this once: Peradventure ten shall be found
there. And he said, I will not destroy it for ten's sake.
—Genesis 18:32 (KJV)

The friend of God can plead with Him for others.
Perhaps Abraham's height of faith and friendship seems
beyond our little possibilities. Do not be discouraged,
Abraham grew; so may we. He went step by step, not
by great leaps. It is no small thing to be on terms of
friendship with God. (SD 5/9)

*H*eavenly Father, we are grateful that you are not only our Father but
also a friend. We pray we will work on developing that friendship
so like Abraham, we may intercede one for another. Thank you for the
invitation to come and talk with you, amen.

Reflections, Thoughts, and Prayer

_____

_____

_____

_____

_____

_____

October 4

> But the prince of the kingdom of Persia withstood
> me one and twenty days: but, lo, Michael, one
> of the chief princes, came to help me; and I
> remained there with the kings of Persia.
> —Daniel 10:13 (KJV)

Daniel had fasted and prayed twenty-one days, it was not because Daniel was not a good man, nor because his prayer was not right; but it was because of a special attack of Satan. Satan delayed the answer three full weeks. Many a Christian's prayer is hindered by Satan; but you need not fear when your prayers and faith pile up; for after a while they will be like a flood, and will not only sweep the answer through, but will also bring some new accompanying blessing. (Sermon SD)

The enemy knows his time is limited, but he still finds ways to destroy our faith. We give you thanks Jesus, for fighting our battles for us and making sure the blessing you sent has come to us as we persevere in prayer, amen.

Reflections, Thoughts, and Prayer

October 5

Put on the whole armour of God that ye may be
able to stand against the wiles of the devil.
—Ephesians 6:11 (KJV)

Every battle is won or lost long before the battle begins.
(Sun Tzu, *The Art of War*)

*H*eavenly Father, we recognize we are at war with dark spirits all around. We are making a decision to daily dress ourselves with Christ's righteousness and put on the full armor of God so we may be able to stand. We ask for power from on high in Jesus's name, amen.

Reflections, Thoughts, and Prayer

_____

_____

_____

_____

_____

_____

_____

_____

October 6

Keep thy tongue from evil,
and thy lips from speaking guile.
—Psalm 34:13 (KJV)

The power to choose also allows us to choose our words. Speaking in a sharp manner comes easy to the carnal man, but training to speak in a gentle, loving, Christlike way requires the Holy Spirit. It should be the duty of all to refine their tongues so the unkind and harsh speaking may cease and love may prevail.

Heavenly Father, I need to tame my tongue for it can be quite harsh toward others bringing about much destruction. I ask for you Holy Spirit to help me develop the habit of encouraging others and lifting up Christ Jesus. That I will have guidance to know which battles are worth fighting and which I should walk away from is my humble prayer in Jesus's name, amen.

Reflections, Thoughts, and Prayer

October 7

Let your speech be alway with grace, seasoned with salt,
that ye may know how ye ought to answer every man.
—Colossians 4:6 (KJV)

We must be steady in our walk with God. We must choose to do right. We must choose to speak right. God has promised His Holy Spirit to us if we would but ask. Believe and abide in the Lord that His Holy Spirit is working in us. We must pray for a God-fearing attitude so others may be encouraged by our words and gloom may be cast aside when we are present.

Let's use our lips to praise the Lord. As we praise Him, our hearts will be filled with His joy, peace, and love.

Heavenly Father, give us hearts that desire to aim higher in developing better characters to represent you better. We pray this in Jesus's name, amen.

Reflections, Thoughts, and Prayer

_____

_____

_____

_____

_____

_____

_____

October 8

And Moses said, Go not up,
for the LORD is not among you.
—Numbers 14:41–42 (KJV)

*A*t times, we fail to move when God says move and we lose the blessing. Many promises stated in the Bible require some action on our part. When God opens a door, go ahead, for it will not be open forever. Many wait too long on God hoping He will do everything for them, and when they finally decide to move, the door closes.

Heavenly Father, we don't want to make the same mistake the children of Israel made by not going to Canaan when you were clearly with them. We ask for forgiveness for complaining and murmuring against you instead of realizing we have on our side the Creator of this vast world. We desire a clear vision to follow our dreams and make haste at every opportunity you present to us; this we pray in Jesus's name, amen.

Reflections, Thoughts, and Prayer

_____

_____

_____

_____

_____

October 9

Death and life are in the power of the tongue: and
they that love it shall eat the fruit thereof.
—Psalm 18:21 (KJV)

*H*ow many families season the day with gossip! Dissecting our friends'
characters has made it a habit to slander all we agree or disagree
with to the point that gossip is a way of communication. Regardless
who is around, the gossip must go on. God is displeased and finds no
honor in such behavior.

Loving Father, thank you for bearing with humankind for all these
thousands of years. I pray that by the power of your Holy Spirit, I will
breathe new life to all those I know or will come to know. May I use
my tongue to bring life and encouragement to all; I pray in Jesus's name,
amen.

Reflections, Thoughts, and Prayer

_____

_____

_____

_____

_____

_____

_____

October 10

And the LORD went before them by day in a pillar of
a cloud, to lead them the way; and by night in a pillar
of fire, to give them light; to go by day and night.
—Exodus 13:21 (KJV)

Do you see the evidence of God's love? God knows just how much you can handle. He knows when to send you an encouraging word and when to delay an answer to prayer. Just as He led the children of Israel in the wilderness, He is leading you. Look for the evidence of His love and see how He is a refuge, defender, protector, and provider. He becomes all things so you need nothing.

You are such a loving Father protecting, preserving, and guiding your children to the Promised Land. We know that as you were with the children of Israel, you are with us today, amen.

Reflections, Thoughts, and Prayer

_____

_____

_____

_____

_____

_____

_____

October 11

And they shall call his name Emmanuel,
which being interpreted is, God with us.
—Matthew 1:23 (KJV)

The angels love to bow before God; they love to be near Him. They regard communion with God as their highest joy; and yet the children of earth, who need so much the help that God only can give, seem satisfied to walk without the light of His Spirit, the companionship of His presence. (SC 94.1)

*H*eavenly Father, we need your presence in our lives. We remember Calvary and how Jesus has torn down the veil and bridged the gap between humanity and heaven. We thank you for your Holy Spirit, who guides us into all truth. We need you in everything. Thank you for never leaving us or forsaking us, amen.

Reflections, Thoughts, and Prayer

_____

_____

_____

_____

_____

_____

October 12

To every thing there is a season.
—Ecclesiastes 3:1 (KJV)

*W*hether you are entering a trial, going through a trial, or coming out of a trial, nothing is here forever. To everything, there is a season. There is a story of a missionary who received bad news and his spirit was downcast. He went to another missionary looking for comfort. When he entered, he saw a sign that read, "Try Thanksgiving!" He did, and in a moment, every shadow was gone. You should praise God whatever the season because it pleases Him.

Heavenly Father, we believe the testing times are here. Keep us motivated to know that seasons change and that this is the time to sow good for in due season, we will reap what we sow. As we go through the tests of life, may we be encouraged knowing a change in season is coming, amen.

Reflections, Thoughts, and Prayer

_____

_____

_____

_____

_____

_____

_____

October 13

My help cometh from the LORD,
which made heaven and earth.
—Psalm 121:2 (KJV)

*S*omeone heard Luther praying, "Gracious God! What spirit and what faith is there in his expressions! He petitions God with as much reverence as if he were in the Divine presence, and yet with as firm a hope and confidence as he would address a father or friend." What a privilege to all who are sons and daughters of God to call Him Father and to call on Him whenever.

Heavenly Father, without you, we are all helpless and hopeless. We know all our help comes from you. We give you our schedules and activities we have planned today, and we pray we will draw near to you. Because of our carnal nature, we are prone to wander from you. We must know what is right to do. Without you, life has no meaning. Give us your Spirit we ask, amen.

Reflections, Thoughts, and Prayer

_____

_____

_____

_____

_____

October 14

And Saul said unto Samuel, I have sinned: for I have
transgressed the commandment of the LORD, and thy
words: because I feared the people, and obeyed their voice.
—1 Samuel 15:24 (KJV)

We should ask God what we ought to pray for. Some pray for riches and power but finally realize that without God, it's a losing battle. Remember that God has a plan for your life; as He elevates you to higher heights, keep adding in Him and keep seeking Him for guidance and wisdom. This is the only path to success.

Heavenly Father, like Saul, we recognize we have sinned and transgressed your Commandments. We ask for forgiveness, and we ask for your Holy Spirit so we can listen to you and follow you way even when it seems we're the only ones on that path. Do it for all those who desire to be in your kingdom; we pray this in Jesus's name, amen.

Reflections, Thoughts, and Prayer

_____

_____

_____

_____

_____

_____

October 15

> For he maketh his sun to rise on the evil and on the
> good, and sendeth rain on the just and on the unjust.
> —Matthew 5:45 (KJV)

God in His mercy meets the needs of all. Caroline Fry, an unbeliever, prayed, "O God, if thou art a God: I do not love thee I do not want thee, but I am miserable, if there is anything better, give it to me." God forgave her and made her extremely happy; she became fruitful in serving Him. If God answered the prayer of an unbeliever, how much more will He do for you?

Heavenly Father, we do not wish to separate ourselves from you, but because of sin, we react based on what we can see and feel even if it is not pleasing to you. Help us walk and live by faith so we may experience a new, fresh blessing that can come only from you, amen.

Reflections, Thoughts, and Prayer

_____

_____

_____

_____

_____

_____

_____

October 16

Your heart shall rejoice,
and your joy no man taketh from you.
—John 16:22 (KJV)

What season are you in today in your walk with God? God wants us to have joy in Him. We must pray in order to stay connected to Him. Take your all that perplexes you, all your cares and sorrow to Him. He has the answers. He knows just how to comfort you. When you are in God, no one can take your joy, and no matter the season, you can rejoice.

It is so good to be in your presence, heavenly Father. We thank you for the reminder that no one can take away our joy. Today, we want to cultivate the habit of being joyful as we work or play. Having a joyful attitude is magnetic, and we want to attract others for your kingdom. Give us the joy that can come only from you until our cup is overflowing we pray, amen.

Reflections, Thoughts, and Prayer

_____

_____

_____

_____

_____

_____

October 17

Having done all, to stand.
—Ephesians 6:13 (KJV)

You need not go to the ends of the earth for wisdom, for God is near. It is not the capabilities you now possess or ever will have that will give you success. It is that which the Lord can do for you. (COL 146.4)

Heavenly Father, though we may not see or feel that our circumstances are changing, we believe that you started to work in our favor the minute we prayed. We are standing in faith waiting for terrific results because you are a great and awesome God able to exceed our expectations. Glory be to Christ for His great sacrifice that makes it possible to have access to you. We ask for strength from your Holy Spirit to stand, smile, and be joyful as we accomplish our daily tasks and give the entire honor to you, amen.

Reflections, Thoughts, and Prayer

_____

_____

_____

_____

_____

October 18

That thou stir up the gift of God, which is in thee.
—2 Timothy 1:6 (KJV)

God has given to everyone a talent for which He can be honored. Do not put your trust in your gift; instead put your trust in the Giver. Let God do for you what you cannot do for yourself.

Heavenly Father, you have given us great talents we need to stir within us to get it out to glorify your holy name. At times, we lack motivation, vision, and encouragement, but we know by your Holy Spirit, we can accomplish what you have put within us. We pray for guidance and opportunity today, amen.

Reflections, Thoughts, and Prayer

_____

_____

_____

_____

_____

_____

_____

_____

October 19

Iron sharpeneth iron; so a man sharpeneth
the countenance of his friend.
—Proverbs 27:17 (KJV)

Fill your surroundings with people who are cheery and joyful. You want friends who will pray for you and pray with you. As you are influencing them, they are influencing you whether for good or evil.

Heavenly Father, today, I give you thanks for friends who continue to sharpen my mind and life for the better. Help me reciprocate by making me the best I can be by the power of your Holy Spirit. Help me be an influence for good to all those whose paths cross mine whether for a season or a lifetime. And when my day here on this planet has come to an end, may my heart print remain with them always I ask in Jesus's name, amen.

Reflections, Thoughts, and Prayer

_____

_____

_____

_____

_____

_____

_____

October 20

No weapon that is formed against thee shall prosper; and every tongue that shall rise against thee in judgment thou shalt condemn. This is the heritage of the servants of the LORD, and their righteousness is of me, saith the LORD.
—Isaiah 54:17 (KJV)

The Lord shall fight for you, and ye shall hold your peace. (Ep 196.3)

We acknowledge that we were not created to be defeated but to overcome. We are grateful, O Father, for your fighting power. No matter what is coming our way in this life, we can take courage because it will not prosper. We pray we will hold our peace and remain on your side always because you have the victory and we are choosing to be on the winning side, amen.

Reflections, Thoughts, and Prayer

_____

_____

_____

_____

_____

_____

_____

October 21

LORD, it is nothing with thee to help, whether with
many, or with them that have no power: help us,
O LORD our God; for we rest on thee, and in thy
name we go against this multitude. O LORD, thou
art our God; let not man prevail against thee.
—2 Chronicles 14:11 (KJV)

*D*oubt not the mighty hand of God. Like Paul, when you can see neither sunrise nor sunset, the storm is raging about, reasons have failed you, and even prayer can't seem to loosen the chain of gloom that is the time to trust in God. Keep your eyes fixed on Him.

Heavenly Father, we come in your mighty and powerful name asking you to help us. We look to you because we are no match for the evil one. Our total dependence is on you. We trust in you and wait on you for Christ's sake, amen.

Reflections, Thoughts, and Prayer

_____

_____

_____

_____

_____

_____

October 22

My soul, wait thou only upon God; for
my expectation is from him.
—Psalm 62:5 (KJV)

*G*eorge Muller got his greatest victories because he prayed. Talk less, pray more as you wait.

Heavenly Father, there is so much we can learn just by looking at nature. Today, we are hopeful that at the right time, what you have in store for every one of us will be fulfilled. Our prayer is that we know your will for our lives so we can give our full cooperation. We give you thanks for the many lessons we have gathered from this vast universe, amen.

Reflections, Thoughts, and Prayer

October 23

> But we trusted.
> —Luke 24:21 (KJV)

*H*ave you prayed and prayed and prayed and nothing seems to be happening? Do not allow discouragement to set in. The enemy of souls would be so glad to see he has stolen your joy. Don't give him that satisfaction. This is the time to go to the Bible and repeat the promise you've been praying God for. Believe in God's faithfulness. Count on Him.

Heavenly Father, it's sad when the disciples said "but we trusted." So many of us are on that road where we no longer trust. Today, we are praying for a breakthrough so the fire within may reignite and we will trust once again just as you did for the disciples. We pray for power, strength, joy, and most important, your Holy Spirit. Give us that living faith we pray, amen.

Reflections, Thoughts, and Prayer

_____

_____

_____

_____

_____

_____

October 24

> But without faith it is impossible to please him: for he
> that cometh to God must believe that he is, and that
> he is a rewarder of them that diligently seek him.
> —Hebrews 11:6 (KJV)

We should not present our petitions to God to prove whether He will fulfill His word, but because He will fulfill it; not to prove that He loves us, but because He loves us. "Without faith it is impossible to please Him: for he that cometh to God must believe that He is, and that He is a rewarder of them that diligently seek Him." (DA 125.4)

*L*oving Father, we are so in awe of your love for us. You have given everything for us to have eternal life. Today, we seek your holy presence. We desire to be where you are and to know and love you. Give us a new heart that will yearn for you always we pray, amen.

Reflections, Thoughts, and Prayer

October 25

Is the LORD among us, or not?
—Exodus 17:7 (KJV)

*R*emember what God has done for you. When perplexed on every side, don't doubt Him. Do not entertain unbelief. True faith believes a "thus saith the Lord."

Heavenly Father, we are sorry for doubting you and your love for us. We are not different from the children of Israel; nothing is new under the sun. Daily, we surrender our doubts. Our lives are in your hands, amen.

Reflections, Thoughts, and Prayer

_____

_____

_____

_____

_____

_____

_____

_____

October 26

She said unto them, Call me not Naomi, call me Mara:
for the Almighty hath dealt very bitterly with me.
—Ruth 1:20 (KJV)

*S*atan loves to cast shadows at the feet of the trusting soul. He delights to nag all your senses until it becomes impossible to discern between God and the forces of evil. Do not allow the shadow to set in. Utter words of praise and remind yourself of God's love for you. God worked it out for Naomi even when she had given up; God never gave up. Keep your rightful name. You are a Christian, a follower of the living God.

Loving Father, today, we choose to believe in you. We are putting all our burdens and woes at the altar and believing for your best. Take away the worries and anxieties. And may we keep our God given name so we won't allow bitterness to take root in our hearts like Naomi, amen.

Reflections, Thoughts, and Prayer

_____

_____

_____

_____

_____

_____

October 27

> Many a time have they afflicted me from my
> youth: yet they have not prevailed against me.
> —Psalm 129:2 (KJV)

Let us not make ourselves miserable over tomorrow's burdens. Bravely and cheerfully carry the burdens of today. Today's trust and faith we must have. But we are not asked to live more than a day at a time. He who gives strength for today will give strength for tomorrow. (2MCP 473. 1)

Heavenly Father, we recognize that we are weak, but with you as our Father, we have more strength to conquer anything that comes our way. We want to fight the good fight of faith. When we look at our past, we see how mightily you've shown up for us. Things we used to worry about had a way of working themselves out. We ask that today we will enjoy because you are in charge of today and it will work out, amen.

Reflections, Thoughts, and Prayer

_____

_____

_____

_____

_____

October 28

Take therefore no thought for the morrow: for the
morrow shall take thought for the things of itself.
Sufficient unto the day is the evil thereof.
—Matthew 6:34 (KJV)

*L*et us not make ourselves miserable over tomorrow and all that will
come. Focus on accomplishing the task for today with an attitude
so attractive it spells out F-A-I-T-H. Believe that God will give you
strength for each new day and every new challenge.

Heavenly Father, we know what it is to go through the fire of life.
We also have experienced your abundance. Today, we pray for closeness,
a relationship that will help us to walk and talk with you constantly. We
give you all our burdens, and we accept your peace. We believe in you;
we believe you are working out the details of our lives for a good finish.
May we learn to trust you, amen.

Reflections, Thoughts, and Prayer

_____

_____

_____

_____

_____

_____

October 29

> Consider the work of God: for who can make
> that straight, which he hath made crooked?
> —Ecclesiastes 7:13 (KJV)

Often God seems to place His children in positions of profound difficulty, leading them into a wedge from which there is no escape; contriving a situation which no human judgment would have permitted, had it been previously consulted. The very cloud conducts them thither. You may be thus involved at this very hour. It does seem perplexing and very serious to the last degree, but it is perfectly right. The issue will more than justify Him who has brought you hither. It is a platform for the display of His almighty grace and power. He will not only deliver you; but in doing so, He will give you a lesson that you will never forget, and to which, in many a psalm and song, in after days, you will revert. You will never be able to thank God enough for having done just as He has. (Selected SD)

*H*eavenly Father, we have all experienced your goodness for which we continue to give you thanks. We pray you do it again for us, amen.

Reflections, Thoughts, and Prayer

_____

_____

_____

_____

October 30

> For I know the thoughts that I think toward
> you, saith the LORD, thoughts of peace, and
> not of evil, to give you an expected end.
> —Jeremiah 29:11 (KJV)

*W*hen we fail to trust God and take Him at His word, we dishonor Him. Do not trust in your emotions to know if you believe or not; simply believe.

Loving Father, today, we truly seek to know you and have a relationship with you so deep that we will take you at your word and have the faith of Abraham. You are a loving Father, and you desire the utmost best for those who are called by your name. Forgive us for not trusting you as we should. May today be the beginning of a beautiful friendship between Father and child we pray in Jesus's name, amen.

Reflections, Thoughts, and Prayer

_____

_____

_____

_____

_____

_____

_____

October 31

Say unto them, As truly as I live, saith the LORD,
as ye have spoken in mine ears, so will I do to you.
—Numbers 14:28 (KJV)

A beautiful French hymn I love to sing, "Compte les Bienfaits de Dieu," is translated to count the blessings of God and you will see what a great number it is. We should thank God for His many blessings; we can trust Him as we wait for the next.

Heavenly Father, we thank you for the promise of hearing and answering our prayers. Today, we activate our trust and recommit our lives to you. We ask you to take away all doubts regarding your love for us. We thank you for loving us unconditionally. Give us your Holy Spirit, and thank you for what you have already done. We want to hear from you, amen.

Reflections, Thoughts, and Prayer

_____

_____

_____

_____

_____

_____

_____

November 1

Jesus said, Take ye away the stone. Martha, the sister
of him that was dead, saith unto him, Lord, by this
time he stinketh: for he hath been dead four days.
—John 11:39 (KJV)

*I*t's so good that we have a Father who doesn't operate on our schedule. Even when God seems to be late, He is still on time. In the presence of God is healing. The Giver of life wants to heal you. He wants to breathe life back into you again. Take courage because Jesus is on the way.

Heavenly Father, we recognize that your presence makes the difference. As you resurrected Lazarus, we pray you will resurrect us. Breathe new life into our brokenness and failures. We invite you into our hearts. Bring about a healing so we can be of use to you we pray, amen.

Reflections, Thoughts, and Prayer

November 2

> And Moses stretched out his hand over the sea; and
> the LORD caused the sea to go back by a strong east
> wind all that night, and made the sea dry land, and
> the waters were divided. And the children of Israel
> went into the midst of the sea upon the dry ground.
> —Exodus 14:21–22 (KJV)

*L*iving faith can give thanks for an answer to prayer even when the act itself has not been performed. Faith is the substance of things hoped for when the evidence is not yet seen. Go forward and watch what God will do.

"Go forward!" is the command given. No matter what our woes, we need to go forward knowing you are before us. O heavenly Father, we pause today to meditate on how great you are. You caused the sea to divide so your children could get to dry land. When to us there is no way, we need to look to Jesus, the only way! No matter what we are facing, we want to remember that you are the same God who parted the sea, and may we believe that at just the right time, you will do the same for us, amen.

Reflections, Thoughts, and Prayer

_____

_____

_____

_____

_____

November 3

He said unto them, Why are ye so fearful?
How is it that ye have no faith?
—Mark 4:40 (KJV)

There is no better way to learn faith except by trials. Jesus walked to Calvary carrying the cross and had complete trust in our Father. This is the same place He is asking you to be at this moment, a place where you are completely dependent on God. Have faith that He will see you through. It does no good to put your trust in humanity or seek advice from them. The trial that has brought you to your knees brought you there for you to pray.

Heavenly Father, we give you our fears and perplexities. We ask that we will receive the measure of faith that has been given us for Christ's sake, amen.

Reflections, Thoughts, and Prayer

_____

_____

_____

_____

_____

_____

_____

November 4

According to your faith be it unto you.
—Matthew 9:29 (KJV)

What can the angels of heaven think of poor helpless human beings, who are subject to temptation, when God's heart of infinite love yearns toward them, ready to give them more than they can ask or think, and yet they pray so little and have so little faith? (Pr. 24.3)

Guilty! I am guilty! Lord, forgive me for not tithing my time to you. Today, I want to recommit my life to you and pray because my life depends on it. Mediocre needs to exit my presence so greatness can come in. I pray for increase in health, love, faith, joy, friendship, wealth, ministry, and all that I haven't mentioned. Your promises are true, and I am thankful. In Jesus's name I pray, amen.

Reflections, Thoughts, and Prayer

November 5

Give thanks unto the LORD, call upon his name,
make known his deeds among the people.
—1 Chronicles 16:8 (KJV)

Let us not be always thinking of our wants and never of the benefits we receive. We do not pray any too much, but we are too sparing of giving thanks. We are the constant recipients of God's mercies, and yet how little gratitude we express, how little we praise Him for what He has done for us. (Pr 287.3)

Heavenly Father, we give you thanks for your protection and the protection of our loved ones. Thank you for health, wealth, family, and friends. Thank you for Jesus dying on the cross to set us free. Thank you for the guardian angels who accompany our going out and coming in. Thank you for your love. We praise you and thank you, amen.

Reflections, Thoughts, and Prayer

_____

_____

_____

_____

_____

_____

November 6

Make a joyful noise unto the LORD, all ye lands.
—Psalm 100:1 (KJV)

*S*ing a psalm of praise and thanksgiving unto the Lord. When you praise God, it does wonders for you but even more for those who are around you who may be feeling discouraged and depressed. When we remain on the joyful side, the home is a happy home; the atmosphere is cheery and inviting. Develop the habit of praising God early in the morning, and as the sun begins to rise, the heart is full of heavenly sunshine.

Heavenly Father, we praise you for being a good God! We praise you for all the good you have bestowed on us even when we didn't deserve it or doubted you. Today, we count our blessings and give you all glory and praise, amen.

Reflections, Thoughts, and Prayer

_____

_____

_____

_____

_____

_____

November 7

The thief cometh not, but for to steal, and to kill,
and to destroy: I am come that they might have life,
and that they might have it more abundantly.
—John 10:10 (KJV)

The just shall live by faith, not by feelings. When sorrow enters the heart, continue to rejoice. It's okay to cry, for the warrior is a child fighting the good fight of faith, but praise God through it all. Do not allow your joy to be taken from you. Jesus died so you might have life. What kind of life would it be to go around moping with a sad, long, countenance? Allow the love of Jesus to stir your heart. As you begin to rejoice and give thanks, your mood begins to change and joy begins to flow through you. A more abundant life is what the experience will be.

Thank you, heavenly Father, for sending your only begotten Son so we might have life more abundantly. We take back our hopes, joys, and aspirations. We choose to be joyful and hopeful because Jesus is alive! Hallelujah! Amen.

Reflections, Thoughts, and Prayer

_____

_____

_____

_____

_____

November 8

For the earth is the Lord's, and the fullness thereof.
—1 Corinthians 10:26 (KJV)

*H*ow far can your faith take you? All you desire to do for God, all you desire in this lifetime is based on your faith in God because the earth and all it contains are the Lord's. We are to show the world that we appreciate every ray of God's blessings displayed in our lives.

Allow your faith to have God take you where you never could have dreamed.

Heavenly Father, I ask you to teach me how to pray because I want to pray big, powerful prayers. The world and all in it belongs to you. I see so many beautiful things that show just how full this world is—fruits, veggies, and nuts and all kinds of animals roaming the earth. This world is full of your goodness. I want the maximum joy and opportunities to tell others of your great love to come my way. Please teach me how to pray powerful prayers, amen.

Reflections, Thoughts, and Prayer

_____

_____

_____

_____

_____

_____

November 9

Fear not, little flock; for it is your Father's
good pleasure to give you the kingdom.
—Luke 12:32 (KJV)

The Lord is disappointed when His people place a low estimate upon themselves. He desires His chosen heritage to value themselves according to the price He has placed upon them. God wanted them, else He would not have sent His Son on such an expensive errand to redeem them. He has a use for them, and He is well pleased when they make the very highest demands upon Him, that they may glorify His name. They may expect large things if they have faith in His promises. (ChS 262.1)

Heavenly Father, today, we want to praise you with our lives. We want to declare that you are God merciful and true. We know your promises are true because you are God and cannot lie. We surrender our fears to you, and we are activating our faith because we know whose we are. We dream of the day when we will be with you throughout eternity in the New Jerusalem, amen.

Reflections, Thoughts, and Prayer

_____

_____

_____

_____

November 10

Oh how great is thy goodness, which thou
hast laid up for them that fear thee;
—Psalm 31:19 (KJV)

God has put you where you are for a purpose. Thrive where you are and be cheerful in duty. Whatever you do, do it willingly. Believe that God has you where He's able to best use you. It is good to believe that He is a rewarder of those who seek Him no matter where they are.

Heavenly Father, heaven is full of goodies, and we want all the goodies you have for us collectively and individually. We are in awe of you and all you have created by the power of your Word. We believe you are a rewarder of those who diligently seek you. We want to get closer to you, Father, because we want to be on the winning side of this life and the life to come. As we await your goodness to pour down upon us without measure, we say thank you for the sacrifice of Christ in whose name we ask, amen.

Reflections, Thoughts, and Prayer

_____

_____

_____

_____

_____

November 11

Behold, I will do a new thing; now it shall
spring forth; shall ye not know it?
—Isaiah 43:19 (KJV)

There is no night that will not make way for the day and no darkness that will not yield to the light. God can change a grim situation in an instant. He can do something new for all those who wait upon Him.

Heavenly Father, we know you have the solutions to every problem humanity has ever faced and will face. We are reassured that nothing lasts forever and that at just the right time, you will do something new in our lives. We may not know the day or the hour, but we know in whom we have believed. We wait in faith for Christ's sake, amen.

Reflections, Thoughts, and Prayer

_____

_____

_____

_____

_____

_____

_____

November 12

Casting all your care upon him; for he careth for you.
—1 Peter 5:7 (KJV)

*I*t is possible to live a life in which all cares, anxiety, depression, and gloom can be cast upon Daddy because He cares for you. He is waiting with open arms to carry your load.

Heavenly Father, as I look around, I see evidence of your love on every leaf, in the unique pattern on each snowflake, and the different animals you created and have made provision for. All nature testifies of your love. Today, I cast all my cares on you, and I ask for a life that will testify to others of your love for them. I ask in Jesus's name, amen.

Reflections, Thoughts, and Prayer

_____

_____

_____

_____

_____

_____

_____

_____

November 13

This I recall to my mind, therefore have I hope.
—Lamentations 3:21 (KJV)

We are to remember that the battle belongs to the Lord. When seas of life are stormy and ominous, you can come to God and find refuge. Let Him fight for you. His resources know no limit. Your hope is in God.

Heavenly Father, today, we choose to remember all your mercies and goodness toward us. We remember the many miracles you have worked out for us, and we can't stop talking about your kind thoughts toward us. We are hopeful and know that the best is yet to come, amen.

Reflections, Thoughts, and Prayer

_____

_____

_____

_____

_____

_____

_____

_____

November 14

> Finally, brethren, whatsoever things are true, whatsoever
> things are honest, whatsoever things are just, whatsoever
> things are pure, whatsoever things are lovely, whatsoever
> things are of good report; if there be any virtue,
> and if there be any praise, think on these things.
> —Philippians 4:8 (KJV)

Get into the habit of looking at the silver lining. Look at the brighter side of things, and when you see that ray of sunshine, look at it instead of the gray clouds all around it. The enemy of souls is a keen observer of what it will take to annoy you; he knows just which buttons to push, just who to send your way to take away your peace. If you keep your thoughts on Jesus, Satan will be sorely disappointed that he is limitless at every turn, and the victory shall be yours through Christ Jesus, our Lord and Savior.

Heavenly Father, we are grateful that we have victory over our enemy thanks be to Jesus. Today, we want to meditate on all things that are good because you have given us so much to thank you for. We know you have much more in store for us. We actively choose to activate our faith for Christ's sake, amen.

Reflections, Thoughts, and Prayer

_____

_____

_____

_____

November 15

> For as he thinketh in his heart, so is he.
> —Proverbs 23:7 (KJV)

*O*ne of my favorite quotes from Joyce Meyer is, "Change your stinking thinking." Your thinking has more power over you than you believe: it's the difference between happiness or sadness, success or failure, and sickness or health. All these are affected by your thoughts, and no one can control your thoughts but you. Ask God for His Holy Spirit to help you get victory over your stinking thinking and watch the gray clouds dissipate.

And so today, heavenly Father, we come before you in prayer to think of all the different ways you can bless us and set us free. Help us remain in faith expecting great things because you are too good to be unkind. May we banish all thoughts of discouragement and know that you are on the throne and your heart is toward us, amen.

Reflections, Thoughts, and Prayer

_____

_____

_____

_____

_____

_____

_____

November 16

Judge not, that ye be not judged.
—Matthew 7:1 (KJV)

*A*ll the marvelous attributes of the Godhead are on the side of the weakest believer. Call on the name of Jesus, ask Him for His Holy Spirit, and He will guide and help you overcome the carnal nature that is prone to wander. Connect with heaven in a simple, childlike trust, ask God to help you with self-control, and all the power of heaven will come to your aid.

We are all travelers, dear Father. I am glad you've taught us how to love one another with the same unconditional love you have for us. Help us live as true representatives of your character and help each other to live lives saturated with sections of the fruit of the Spirit I pray, amen.

Reflections, Thoughts, and Prayer

_____

_____

_____

_____

_____

_____

_____

> Pray without ceasing.
> —1 Thessalonians 5:17 (KJV)

Prayer is not only a calling upon God, but also a conflict with Satan. And inasmuch as God is using our intercession as a mighty factor of victory in that conflict, He alone, and not we, must decide when we dare cease from our petitioning. So we dare not stay our prayer until the answer itself has come, Or until we receive the assurance that it will come. More and more, as we live the prayer life, shall we come to experience and recognize this God-given assurance, and know when to rest quietly in it, or when to continue our petitioning until we receive it. (*The Practice of Prayer*)

*H*eavenly Father, there's so much we don't understand about the spirit realm. We pray we will do our part, listen to your voice, trust your leading, and pray until it is granted or we have your peace that it is well. Keep us faithful, amen.

Reflections, Thoughts, and Prayer

_____

_____

_____

_____

_____

November 18

Then said David to the Philistine, Thou comest to me
with a sword, and with a spear, and with a shield: but
I come to thee in the name of the LORD of hosts, the
God of the armies of Israel, whom thou hast defied.
This day will the LORD deliver thee into mine hand.
—1 Samuel 17:45–46 (KJV)

Goliath trusted in his armor. He terrified the armies of
Israel by his defiant, savage boastings, while he made
a most imposing display of his armor, which was his
strength. David, in his humility and zeal for God and
his people, proposed to meet this boaster. Saul consented
and had his own kingly armor placed upon David. But
he would not consent to wear it. He laid off the king's
armor, for he had not proved it. He had proved God
and, in trusting in Him, had gained special victories.
(3T 218.2)

*H*eavenly Father, today, we come in the mighty name of Jesus to say
we will not give up our desires and dreams you have placed in our
hearts. Like David, we will look our giants in the face and in the name
of the Lord get the victory that we have been praying for, amen.

Reflections, Thoughts, and Prayer

_____

_____

_____

_____

November 19

The steps of a good man are ordered by the
LORD: and he delighteth in his way.
—Psalm 37:23 (KJV)

The just shall live by faith. When you've done what God has asked in obeying Him and it seems nothing is changing, this is when to apply the quote "The just shall live by faith." Remember that as His child, God is leading you step by step. There are times when you won't understand how He is leading you or what His purpose is, but trust Him amid it all. Trust and obey.

Heavenly Father, we realize that these last days are times to live by faith knowing without a doubt that you are leading your children. We have experienced divine connections and intervention in the past, and we can be sure that at just the right time we will experience divine connections again whether in wealth, health, or relationships. May we keep trust in you now until the end of days fearing no man and no circumstances. We ask this in Jesus's name, amen.

Reflections, Thoughts, and Prayer

November 20

Nevertheless the people be strong that dwell in the land,
and the cities are walled, and very great: And Caleb stilled
the people before Moses, and said, Let us go up at once,
and possess it; for we are well able to overcome it. But
the men that went up with him said, we be not able to
go up against the people; for they are stronger than we.
—Numbers 13:28–31 (KJV)

The same power that sustained Caleb and Joshua with courage to meet the challenge of the day is available to you also. Out of so many, only two remembered the presence of God was with them. Today, you can be one of the two.

Heavenly Father, today, we want to be like Caleb and Joshua and focus on the promise rather than the problem. Our circumstances are never bigger than you, our Father and our God. It's due time to shake off the negativity and the doubts and claim the desires you have placed in our hearts. May we develop an attitude like that of Caleb by the power of your Holy Spirit trusting you even when things seem impossible. We ask this in Jesus's name, amen.

Reflections, Thoughts, and Prayer

_____

_____

_____

_____

_____

November 21

Now faith is the substance of things hoped
for, the evidence of things not seen.
—Hebrews 11:1 (KJV)

When the mountains of difficulties challenge your faith, remember that God can use it for your good because all things work together for good to those who love God.

Opposition is essential for building our faith. These mountainous obstacles are here to empower us, to test our faith, and bring us higher. This is the time to trust in God and in the power of His Spirit.

Loving Father, help us shake off the doubts surrounding our lives. We need to exercise our faith in you by facing the challenges of life with joy and song in our hearts. Let us not question the places in our lives where you have closed that chapter; help us to move forward in life trusting you are a loving Father who desires the very best for His children. Today is a new day for a new attitude. We pray your Holy Spirit will continue to be in our midst in Jesus's name, amen.

Reflections, Thoughts, and Prayer

_____

_____

_____

_____

_____

_____

November 22

Looking unto Jesus the author and finisher of our faith.
—Hebrews 12:2 (KJV)

S ome of life's greatest blessings we would not have known if not for the trials we endured. If we meet hardships in our Christian pathway, we should look to Jesus, the Alpha and Omega, our beginning and end.

Heavenly Father, today, we want to remember that you are the Author and Finisher of our lives. We want to focus on your greatness and how you have led us to higher grounds knowing you are guiding our every step. Instead of focusing on our problems, help us focus on your goodness because you are the God who parted the Red Sea who will do more than we can imagine as we put our trust in you this happy day, amen.

Reflections, Thoughts, and Prayer

_____

_____

_____

_____

_____

_____

November 23

It is good for me to draw near to God: I have put my trust
in the Lord GOD, that I may declare all thy works.
—Psalm 73:28 (KJV)

True success in any line of work is not the result of
chance or accident or destiny. It is the outworking of
God's providences, the reward of faith and discretion,
of virtue and perseverance. Fine mental qualities and
a high moral tone are not the result of accident. God
gives opportunities; success depends upon the use made
of them. (CSA 56.1)

Heavenly Father, we pray for that persevering spirit. Give us wisdom
to see which doors you are opening for us and the boldness to go
in that direction. We also need wisdom to see which doors you have
closed and courage to persevere in the direction you are leading us even
when it's not all too clear for us. May we persevere until we reach the
highest level of success this life can bring. We trust in your leading for
Christ's sake, amen.

Reflections, Thoughts, and Prayer

_____

_____

_____

_____

_____

November 24

By faith they passed through the Red sea as by dry land.
—Hebrews 11:29 (KJV)

One of my favorite chapters in the Bible is Hebrews 11, the chapter on faith. It takes you to the Faith Hall of Fame and describes each person of faith and what they worked. Each Hall of Famer had severe trials over which they were victorious only by faith. The greater your faith, the higher Satan aims to attack, but God remains greater still. By faith, you too can see the impossible become possible.

Heavenly Father, today, you bid us go forward. You've asked us not to worry about the Red Sea or our circumstances before us or what is behind us but to go forward because you, Almighty, are with us. As we move forward by faith, we too will cross on dry land and have the victory. Keep us faithful, amen.

Reflections, Thoughts, and Prayer

_____

_____

_____

_____

_____

_____

_____

November 25

And I will bless them that bless thee, and curse him that
curseth thee: and in thee shall all families of
the earth be blessed.
—Genesis 12:3 (KJV)

*R*est on the Word of God. If He has blessed you, no one can curse you. Balaam experienced that when he tried to curse the children of Israel, but the power of God rested on him, and he in turn blessed the children instead of cursing them. God is delighted when we exercise our faith and take Him at His word; He is then able to bless us and be glorified.

Heavenly Father, you are truly amazing at turning our situations around to be blessings for us even when the enemy meant to harm and destroy us. You are a wonderful Father who keeps His promises from generation to generation. Blessed are we for all to see that we are blessed indeed in Jesus's name, amen.

Reflections, Thoughts, and Prayer

_____

_____

_____

_____

_____

_____

November 26

Glory ye in his holy name: let the heart of them
rejoice that seek the Lord.
—1 Chronicles 16:10 (KJV)

*I*sn't it strange that when perplexities and difficulties arise, we go for help to others who are no wiser or stronger than ourselves while Jesus is waiting for us to come to Him, who is able to supply all our needs? We need to learn how to take everything to God in prayer. There, we will find peace, strength, and rest for our weary souls. God can answer all our questions; He can show us a way when no one else sees a way. Go to God in faith doubting nothing; watch God do amazing things.

Heavenly Father, we are seeking a deeper walk with you. We are knocking on heaven's door asking for your divine intervention in our lives. Without you, we can do nothing. We desire to do great things to honor you; that is our earnest plea in Jesus's name, amen.

Reflections, Thoughts, and Prayer

> Arise, shine.
> —Isaiah 60:1 (KJV)

*A*braham was asked to arise and go to a place where he had no relatives for his inheritance. He obeyed. It is no easy task to be in the army of God. He will not lead you as you expect to be led; He will not do things as you imagined they would be done. He may take you on a journey you would never have envisioned, but our God knows no fear, and He expects you to fear nothing but to arise in obedience and follow Him.

Heavenly Father, you have asked us to rise and shine. Help us eliminate all the negative things the enemy keeps our focus on, and let us look upward to King Jesus, who is ever victorious and reigns forever and in whose name we pray, amen.

Reflections, Thoughts, and Prayer

_____

_____

_____

_____

_____

_____

_____

November 28

> For I am not come to call the righteous,
> but sinners to repentance.
> —Matthew 9:13 (KJV)

*E*very son and daughter of Adam may come to Jesus—the way, the truth, and the life. He wants all to repent and take on His name. Drugs and alcohol can do nothing to numb the pain; healing for your soul can be found only in Christ Jesus. Stop swimming against the current; come to the Master of the sea. When He speaks, the waters listen. In every created thing, we see God with us.

What a comfort to know you are always here with us and nothing happens to your children without your approval. It is good to know that you understand our trials and circumstances and that You will never leave or forsake us, amen.

Reflections, Thoughts, and Prayer

_____

_____

_____

_____

_____

_____

November 29

> A good name is rather to be chosen than great riches.
> —Proverbs 22:1 (KJV)

*A*braham was not discouraged when he was told he would bear seed even in his old age because he wasn't looking at the deadness of his body but to the almighty God of the universe.

You are a chosen child of God. You have His name, and all things are possible with God.

I praise your holy name for the influence your Word has on my life and the decisions I make. Loving Father, I pray I may be impact others for the good and for your kingdom. I ask that those that will cross my paths will help me to be more like my elder brother, Jesus Christ, and may the sweet, sweet anointing of your Holy Spirit be felt wherever I may go so a desire to know more about you will stir in those whose paths I have crossed. Help me live accordingly in Jesus's name I pray, amen.

Reflections, Thoughts, and Prayer

_____

_____

_____

_____

_____

_____

> You prepare a table before me in the
> presence of my enemies.
> —Psalm 23:5 (KJV)

To the reproaches of his enemies who taunted him with the weakness of his cause, Luther answered: "Who knows if God has not chosen and called me, and if they ought not to fear that, by despising me, they despise God Himself? Moses was alone at the departure from Egypt; Elijah was alone in the reign of King Ahab; Isaiah alone in Jerusalem; Ezekiel alone in Babylon. … God never selected as a prophet either the high priest or any other great personage; but ordinarily He chose low and despised men, once even the shepherd Amos." (CG 142.3)

*I*t may seem I am alone, but I know Jesus is by my side and will never leave or forsake me. Thank you for the many blessings you've prepared for me in the presence of my enemies. May I live to please you as Luther did is my prayer in Jesus's name, amen.

Reflections, Thoughts, and Prayer

_____

_____

_____

_____

_____

December 1

Draw nigh to God, and he will draw nigh to you.
—James 4:8 (KJV)

Are you seeking for a renewal in your religious life with God? Draw closer to Him. Come to Him, the Bread of life and drink from the One who can give you water where you will never thirst again. When you seek God with praise and thanksgiving, He will give you freshness. Your spiritual life will improve tenfold and power from heaven will be yours for the taking. It is no small thing to know God. He will be the first friend you seek in time of trouble. He will be the Friend to tell your good news to. You will talk to Him as you talk to a friend.

My loving Father in heaven, you are worthy of praise for you are good and your mercy endures forever and ever. I'm thankful that your loving arms are longing to draw me closer to you. Create in me a new heart to love you and follow your way, not humanities'. This I pray in Jesus's name, amen.

Reflections, Thoughts, and Prayer

_____

_____

_____

_____

_____

_____

December 2

Humble yourselves in the sight of the Lord,
and he shall lift you up.
—James 4:10 (KJV)

*H*ow different and how much more joyful would our lives be if we humbled ourselves and allowed the Almighty to lift us up? If we paused daily to take the focus off ourselves and looked to Jesus, we would find reasons to sing God's praises. Let us praise God for how He will lift us up when we humble ourselves. Let's ask for His Holy Spirit to help us afflict our souls seeking first in foremost the kingdom of God.

Loving Father, I come because I need your Holy Spirit to help me humble myself. I am full of pride, greed, and selfishness. I desire to be more like Jesus and less like me. I want to be used by you to finish this great work I pray in Jesus's name, amen.

Reflections, Thoughts, and Prayer

_____

_____

_____

_____

_____

_____

December 3

For the Son of man is not come to destroy men's lives,
but to save them.
—Luke 9:56 (KJV)

The ministry of sorrow can bring about the most fruit when you learn to call on the name that matters, the name of Jesus. It is not enough to pray in His name; you must know Him, His ways, His leading, and His voice. You must know the person behind the name.

Heavenly Father, we praise you because you are good, true, and holy. You sent Jesus to save us from the enemy; we praise you for that. No matter what today may bring, we know victory is ours in Jesus's name, amen.

Reflections, Thoughts, and Prayer

_____

_____

_____

_____

_____

_____

_____

_____

December 4

> For they considered not the miracle of the
> loaves: for their heart was hardened.
> —Mark 6:52 (KJV)

*D*on't make the miracles God has done in your life of no effect. Don't disregard His benediction as common, everyday events. Look for glimpses of God daily, and daily give thanks and sing His praises.

Heavenly Father, I praise you for all you have blessed me with and the trials you have seen me through. I desire to have power, but I need your Holy Spirit. I need to be converted anew. Search me, my Lord, and make me what I ought to be. Let me not harden my heart and treat the extraordinary gifts you've given me as anything ordinary. May I continue to praise you throughout the end of eternity I pray in Jesus's holy name, amen.

Reflections, Thoughts, and Prayer

_____

_____

_____

_____

_____

_____

_____

December 5

> Then Peter said unto them, Repent, and be baptized
> every one of you in the name of Jesus Christ for
> the remission of sins, and ye shall receive the gift
> of the Holy Ghost ... and the same day there were
> added unto them about three thousand souls.
> —Acts 2:38, 41 (KJV)

The psalmist reminds us, "The secret of the Lord is with them that fear Him." Like the apostles, we need the Holy Spirit to help us discern God's leading and the part He is calling us to do in this great work. We need the Holy Spirit to help us grow so our experiences will be richer than before. We need the Holy Spirit to help us see the doors of opportunity to reach one for His kingdom. We need the power of His Holy Spirit.

Heavenly Father, show me my sins so I may repent and be a vessel ready to receive the power of the Holy Ghost. I pray this in the mighty name of Jesus, amen.

Reflections, Thoughts, and Prayer

_____

_____

_____

_____

_____

_____

December 6

But ye, brethren, are not in darkness, that
that day should overtake you as a thief.
—1 Thessalonians 5:4 (KJV)

There is a limit to sin, and sin has almost reached its limit. Terror and confusion are all around. To be able to stand, put on the whole armor of God. Let Him be your Commander in Chief. As He gives the orders, follow them. The battle is soon finished.

Heavenly Father, we magnify your name and thank you for sharing in your Word the time in which we are living. Help us to prioritize our minds to what will lead us to heaven. May we keep our eyes on the lovely Jesus and search the scripture prayerfully so nothing will be a surprise to those who are called by your name, amen.

Reflections, Thoughts, and Prayer

_____

_____

_____

_____

_____

_____

_____

December 7

These are they which came out of great
tribulation, and have washed their robes, and
made them white in the blood of the Lamb.
—Revelation 7:14 (KJV)

*L*et's strive to be among those who have come out of great tribulations and into great jubilation. We must keep our eyes fixed on heaven. Jesus went to prepare a place for us, and He is coming soon to take us home never to part from Him again. What a beautiful day that will be. Imagine singing with the angels of heaven beholding the Lamb of God. Heaven is cheap enough for the little discomfort we are going through.

Loving Savior, I want to be a part of that number. I want to be one of those who have come through great tribulation into great jubilation. I pray for vision of heavenly things in Jesus's name, amen.

Reflections, Thoughts, and Prayer

_____

_____

_____

_____

_____

_____

December 8

Finally, my brethren, be strong in the Lord,
and in the power of his might.
—Ephesians 6:10 (KJV)

The command is given: "Men ought always to pray … and not to faint." Prayer connects you directly to heaven to face any obstacle, any person, and any evil. The strength of the Lord is yours. The days ahead are treacherous. Many will be sifted out; many who thought they had light will find themselves in darkness. But as His child, you can find rest in the Lord.

I need your strength, Father; I need your Holy Spirit. I pray that when the sifting takes place, I will be found to be one of the just. I pray for strength to walk in the light that have been given me, and no matter what may be happening to the right or the left of me, I will stand firmly on your Living Word and not be shaken or moved. I pray this in Jesus's name, amen.

Reflections, Thoughts, and Prayer

_____

_____

_____

_____

_____

_____

December 9

> For we wrestle not against flesh and blood, but against
> principalities, against powers, against the rulers of the
> darkness of this world, against spiritual
> wickedness in high places.
> —Ephesians 6:12 (KJV)

Sing God's praises and watch the fog lift,
Sing God's praises, enjoy your life, His gift.
Worry less and praise Him more for He is ever near,
As you sing God's praises, anxieties disappear.

*D*on't let your song be taken from you. If Satan knows he can't have you, he will do things to annoy you and steal your peace. When that happens, praise the Lord and watch the shackles fall.

Heavenly Father, we call on you today and every day because you are our all and all. Our desire is to live lives that will honor you and make you proud. Give us that perseverance spirit we pray in Jesus's name, amen.

Reflections, Thoughts, and Prayer

_____

_____

_____

_____

_____

December 10

> We have also a more sure word of prophecy; whereunto ye
> do well that ye take heed, as unto a light that shineth in a
> dark place, until the day dawn,
> and the day star arise in your hearts.
> —2 Peter 1:19 (KJV)

To take God at His word requires discipline of faith. Through the prophets, God has revealed to us how it all began and how it will all end. Though you've prayed and you've prayed but nothing seems to be happening, I encourage you to not faint. Now is the time to pray. Jesus is coming again. All He said would happen will happen. The period of grace is given to us to put oil in our lamps so like the five wise virgins, we may be ready when the bridegroom comes.

Help me never lose sight of you, dear Jesus, for the consequences would be too great. Thank you for being in charge of my life, the events of the time, and the universe. My trust is in you, Lord, amen.

Reflections, Thoughts, and Prayer

_____

_____

_____

_____

_____

_____

December 11

By humility and the fear of the LORD are riches,
and honour, and life.
—Proverbs 22:4 (KJV)

Life's best things—simplicity, honesty, truthfulness, purity, unsullied integrity—cannot be bought or sold; they are as free to the ignorant as to the educated, to the black man as to the white man, to the humble peasant as to the king upon his throne. Humble workers, who do not trust in their own strength, but who labor in simplicity, trusting always in God, will share in the joy of the Saviour. Their persevering prayers will bring souls to the cross. (7T 27.2)

*H*eavenly Father, I thank you for your peace. I desire to humble myself by the power of your Holy Spirit and to life a good life, one that will glorify you now and in heaven. Give me your Holy Spirit I pray in Jesus's name, amen.

Reflections, Thoughts, and Prayer

_____

_____

_____

_____

_____

December 12

My son forget not my law; but let thine
heart keep my commandments.
—Proverbs 3:1 (KJV)

When God asks you to do something, obey Him quickly. Don't stop to reason if you should or not giving way to disobedience. Be instant in season lest you lose the opportunity to obey and temptation leads you astray.

Heavenly Father, your Commandments are sweet and bring about peace, joy, and love. I pray that like David, I will hide your Word in my heart so I might not sin against you. I pray to obey you so I may reap the many blessings that come with being your child by the power of the Holy Ghost. I know I can in Jesus's name, amen.

Reflections, Thoughts, and Prayer

_____

_____

_____

_____

_____

_____

_____

December 13

And He said to them, "He who has ears to hear,
let him hear!"
—Mark 4:9 (KJV)

*M*artin Luther said, "A true believer will crucify the question, 'Why?' He will obey without questioning." God is asking you to leave it all with Him as you tell of His redeeming love to the world. Listen to that still, small voice and obey.

Loving Redeemer, today, I desire to cooperate with your Holy Spirit to work out the flaws in my character that may be keeping others from coming to know the lovely Jesus. I don't want to be powerless or purposeless because I know like every parent, you too have a plan for my life. I want to live that life to the fullest in Jesus's name, amen.

Reflections, Thoughts, and Prayer

_____

_____

_____

_____

_____

_____

_____

December 14

Let the beauty of the LORD our God be upon us.
—Psalm 90:17 (KJV)

*L*ook around and see the beauty of the Lord. The rising and setting of the sun, the majestic roar of the lion, the stillness of the brook, all testify of His love. Most beautiful of all is a character reflecting Christ; it can pierce more hearts than a hundred sermons.

Heavenly Father, you are beautiful and majestic. I want to share your goodness all around the world. I pray for a Christlike character. I want others to see your beauty in me today and every day. Help me to develop the fruit of the Spirit—gentleness, joy and love I pray in Jesus's name, amen.

Reflections, Thoughts, and Prayer

_____

_____

_____

_____

_____

_____

_____

_____

December 15

The angel of the LORD encampeth round about
them that fear him, and delivereth them.
—Psalm 34:7 (KJV)

Could men see with heavenly vision, they would behold
companies of angels that excel in strength stationed
about those who have kept the word of Christ's patience.
With sympathizing tenderness, angels have witnessed
their distress and have heard their prayers. They are
waiting the word of their Commander to snatch them
from their peril. But they must wait yet a little longer.
The people of God must drink of the cup and be baptized
with the baptism. (GC 630.2)

Thank you, Father, for your holy angels. They are a constant force by
our side keeping us out of harm's way and ministering to us when
we've reached out limits with the burdens of life. There is no need to
fear, but help us believe is our prayer in Jesus's name, amen.

Reflections, Thoughts, and Prayer

_____

_____

_____

_____

_____

_____

December 16

Let the words of my mouth, and the meditation of my
heart, be acceptable in thy sight, O LORD,
my strength, and my redeemer.
—Psalm 19:14 (KJV)

*O*ur hearts should be full of the language of Canaan, a language so
pure and loving that it blesses those who are in our midst. Give
God your heart; let Him keep it pure. Let God mold you and fashion
you into His likeness. He will give you His strength and take away
your weakness. Give Him your sins, and He will give you the robe of
Christ's righteousness.

Lord, search my heart; take away anything in it that is not like you
and fill it with your goodness until my cup is overflowing with your love,
truth, and mercy. I pray this for Christ's sake, amen.

Reflections, Thoughts, and Prayer

_____

_____

_____

_____

_____

_____

_____

December 17

Seek ye the LORD, all ye meek of the earth.
—Zephaniah 2:3 (KJV)

Seek God first thing in the morning. Open your heart to Him. Praise and thank Him for new experiences and new blessings. Praise Him for provisions He has made to meet the day's challenges. Tell Him your desires and give Him your worries. Your prayer should be fresh, new; daily seek the Lord while He may be found.

Father of humanity, great God of Israel, thank you for your gift of righteousness. We accept your forgiveness and pray that by the power of your Holy Spirit, we wear the valuable robe with dignity to be called sons and daughters of the true God. We seek you to give you praise and honor in Jesus's name, amen.

Reflections, Thoughts, and Prayer

_____

_____

_____

_____

_____

_____

_____

December 18

And many nations shall come, and say, Come, and
let us go up to the mountain of the LORD, and to
the house of the God of Jacob; and he will teach
us of his ways, and we will walk in his paths.
—Micah 4:2 (KJV)

*M*ake God part of your routine. Like Daniel, go to God alone in prayer regularly. You will find strength in Him to complete the tasks of the day; you will fail if you expect to start the day in your own strength. With His holy scripture in hand and an open heart, ask God to not only teach you His way but also give you a love to do His will.

My Savior, my desire is to walk in your holy name forever. I don't just want to praise you with lip service; I want my life to reflect you inside and out. I want my private and public life to reflect you and your goodness. Take my heart and cleanse it thoroughly I pray in Jesus's name, amen.

Reflections, Thoughts, and Prayer

_____

_____

_____

_____

_____

_____

December 19

> Dear children, let us not love with words or
> tongue but with actions and in truth.
> —1 John 3:18 (KJV)

*A*ctions speak louder than words. What love would take on the sinful nature of humanity, be humiliated, rejected, and killed so you might have eternal life? If Christ would go through all this to show you how much He loves you, why do you doubt Him so? Let not your heart be troubled; the victory is yours through Christ Jesus, who so loved you that He gave His life for you. There's no greater action than this, no greater love.

Heavenly Father, I thank you for the opportunity given to humanity to work with you in revealing your character. I pray for strength to overcome sin today by the power of your Holy Spirit in Jesus's name, amen.

Reflections, Thoughts, and Prayer

December 20

For I am not ashamed of the gospel of Christ.
—Romans 1:16 (KJV)

The disciples went forth with a zeal and boldness to proclaim to the world the gospel of Jesus Christ. "He is risen"—you can hear them shouting the good news with joy in their hearts. We need the faith and the boldness they showed; we need the power of the Holy Spirit. Let the world know that Jesus saves.

I desire to be a living epistle reaching all humanity for your heavenly kingdom by my lifestyle. Father, I pray for that childlike faith that believes all things from your Living Word. I await the many blessings you have in store for me as I praise your name when in the valley as well as when on the mountaintop in Jesus's name, amen.

Reflections, Thoughts, and Prayer

_____

_____

_____

_____

_____

_____

_____

December 21

As it is written, the just shall live by faith.
—Romans 1:17 (KJV)

At every corner in this walk of life awaits a situation to rob you of your triumphs and peace of mind if you allow it. Satan is ever seeking opportunities to discourage, confuse, tempt, and destroy you. Have an active faith in God. He can change any situation in a moment's notice. Faith can change anything. No matter how grim or how dark things are, pray and believe that God can change it. Faith sees what others cannot see and hears what others cannot hear. Don't let discouragement deplete you of your faith. When no one else believes, remember you are to walk by faith.

Heavenly Father, this morning, I pray that nothing will take priority in my life but the lovely Jesus. I ask that I number my days to make the most of the time given me to live a life guided by your Holy Spirit. I pray this in Jesus's name, amen.

Reflections, Thoughts, and Prayer

_____

_____

_____

_____

_____

_____

Though he slay me, yet will I trust in him.
—Job 13:15 (KJV)

*J*ob's faith was not moved by all the calamities that befell him. His faith was strong in the Lord. The enemy brought him to the lowest point that any human being could manage, yet Job trusted God. His words of encouragement still ring true today: "The Lord gives, the Lord takes away, bless be His name." Job was willing to follow God wherever he was led even to the grave. It's faith that keeps one praising when all is dark believing that God can cause the sun to shine again.

Heavenly Father, it is good to trust in you because you are good, loyal, and loving. I pray for a fresh outpouring of your Holy Spirit to enable me to live the best life you have for me no matter what may come. And like Job, I can one day say, though He slay me, yet will I trust in you, amen.

Reflections, Thoughts, and Prayer

_____

_____

_____

_____

_____

_____

December 23

And it came to pass, that after three days they found him.
—Luke 2:46 (KJV)

*I*magine a day without Jesus. No, I can't. Yet, for three days, Joseph and Mary couldn't find Jesus. Dear one, stay close to your Redeemer. Each time your heart wanders from Him when you neglect to pray, it will take many days to find your way back to Him and to reestablish the relationship you once had and get back your peace. Keep a fixed eye on Jesus and feed on His faithfulness.

Heavenly Father, there is no life without Jesus—the Way, Truth, and Life. I pray I may be on guard praying without ceasing lest I too like Mary and Joseph lose Jesus. The consequence would be too much to bear. For Jesus is my all and all, amen.

Reflections, Thoughts, and Prayer

_____

_____

_____

_____

_____

_____

_____

_____

December 24

For precept must be upon precept, precept upon precept;
line upon line, line upon line; here a little,
and there a little.
—Isaiah 28:10 (KJV)

The Bible explains itself. One passage will be a significant key to understanding other passages. Compare various texts relating to the same subject and God's Holy Spirit will shed light and the true meaning of the scripture will be made plain. Learn to study the precious Word of God, put it in your heart, and in times of despair, recite a verse and find solace there. God has given us His Word for an example where we can see ordinary people doing extraordinary things when they trusted God. You too can do amazing things for God by God.

Heavenly Father, we are in need of truth. This world is moving fast toward evil, and we are sleeping and listening to humanity instead of delving into the Word prayerfully so we may have a clear understanding of a "thus said the Lord." Give us your Holy Spirit we pray in Jesus's name, amen.

Reflections, Thoughts, and Prayer

_____

_____

_____

_____

_____

December 25

Therefore, brethren, stand fast, and hold the traditions,
which ye have been taught, whether by word, or our epistle.
—2 Thessalonians 2:15 (KJV)

H old fast to the principles of the Word. If God, the Captain of our souls, is with us, we shall withstand the time of trouble that is to come upon this earth like no one has seen. The fruit of the Spirit are not developed by chance. Regularly seek the Word to see what God would have you to do in every facet of life and then do it.

O God, the trials are fiery and to us seem impossible, but today, we activate our faith to stand up for truth and make it clear we are on your side. Let our influence be one that is strong and solid in Jesus. We're not able to stand without your Holy Spirit. Give us your Spirit we pray in Jesus's name, amen.

Reflections, Thoughts, and Prayer

_____

_____

_____

_____

_____

_____

_____

December 26

Therefore whosoever heareth these sayings of mine, and
doeth them, I will liken him unto a wise man, which built
his house upon a rock: And every one that heareth these
sayings of mine, and doeth them not, shall be likened
unto a foolish man, which built his house upon the sand.
—Matthew 7:24, 26 (KJV)

*L*et's build our house on the Rock. Jesus is that Rock, and when the
tempests of life rage, our house built on Christ will stand firm.
When you follow your own path and go in your own strength, you are
not equipped to handle the storms of this life and failure is inevitable.
Come to the Rock that is higher than us.

In this parable two classes are brought to view, —those
who hear the words of Christ, and do them; and those
who hear, and do not. God has a standard of righteousness
by which he measures character. This standard is his holy
law, which is given to us as a rule of life. (ST 833)

Heavenly Father, we want to be like the wise man who built his
house on the rock, but like the foolish man, at times we want what the
world says is best. We are easily influenced. Forgive us; with your Holy
Spirit, may we choose better we pray today, amen.

Reflections, Thoughts, and Prayer

_____

_____

_____

_____

December 27

The fear of the LORD is the beginning of wisdom:
and the knowledge of the holy is understanding.
—Proverbs 9:10 (KJV)

C haracter building is the greatest task given along with knowledge of God. Know that God is majestic, holy, and good. We should come into His presence with awe and reverence. Take time to communicate to Him in understanding heavenly things. Strive to make heaven your home.

Loving Father, this morning, we come because we need wisdom to distinguish between the holy and the profane. We need a cleaning starting from our inside out. We need Jesus. We come because we want a powerful prayer life. Please show us whatever is hindering power when we pray so we might cooperate with your Holy Spirit to change and reflect more of your character. We pray this in Jesus's name, amen.

Reflections, Thoughts, and Prayer

_____

_____

_____

_____

_____

_____

December 28

The eyes of the LORD are in every place,
beholding the evil and the good.
—Proverbs 15:3 (KJV)

If the heart is right, your words, your dress, your acts will all be right. True godliness is lacking. I would not dishonor my Master so much as to admit that a careless, trifling, prayerless person is a Christian. No; a Christian has victory over his besetments, over his passions. There is a remedy for the sin-sick soul. (MYP 131.2)

*L*oving Father, we need your Holy Spirit. We need a clean heart. We need to develop a love for you. Father, as the year is coming to an end, we want to reflect on our growth as Christians. Did we impact anyone? Did we get closer to you by studying and praying? Did we learn your will for our lives? We need power. We need you, Lord, today, amen.

Reflections, Thoughts, and Prayer

_____

_____

_____

_____

_____

_____

December 29

And I saw as it were a sea of glass mingled with fire:
and them that had gotten the victory over the beast,
and over his image, and over his mark, and over the
number of his name, stand on the sea of glass, having
the harps of God. And they sing the song of Moses the
servant of God, and the song of the Lamb, saying, Great
and marvelous are thy works, Lord God Almighty;
just and true are thy ways, thou King of saints.
—Revelation 15:2–3 (KJV)

God is always a majority. When the sound of the last
trump shall penetrate the prison house of the dead, and
the righteous shall come forth with triumph, exclaiming,
"O death, where is thy sting? O grave, where is thy
victory?" Standing then with God, with Christ, with
the angels, and with the loyal and true of all ages, the
children of God will be far in the majority. (AA 590)

*O*h my God, what a day it will be when Jesus will come and we will
be with Him forever. Today, we pray for victory over self. Help us,
Father; help us today for Christ's sake, amen.

Reflections, Thoughts, and Prayer

_____

_____

_____

_____

December 30

> Let us hear the conclusion of the whole matter: Fear God,
> and keep his commandments: for this is
> the whole duty of man.
> —Ecclesiastes 12:13 (KJV)

*C*hrist prayed for Peter that his faith not fail him; likewise, we ought to pray one for another in these trying times that our faith remains firm in Jesus.

Know your duty as an ambassador to the New Jerusalem. Take time to have one-to-one time with your heavenly Father and fellowship with Him daily. Make it your goal to be like Daniel praying three times a day. Stay connected with heaven and victories upon victories shall be yours for the taking.

Heavenly Father, we worship you because you deserve our worship. We ask to develop a fear of and reverence for you. We live in a secular world that promotes every uncouth thing and calls it good; it's becoming more difficult to reverence your name and keep your way holy. We are in need of your Holy Spirit. Fill us with a love for you we pray in Jesus's name, amen.

Reflections, Thoughts, and Prayer

_____

_____

_____

_____

_____

December 31

And the Lord direct your hearts into the love of God,
and into the patient waiting for Christ. The grace
of our Lord Jesus Christ be with you all, amen.
—2 Thessalonians 3:5 (KJV)

We are pilgrims in God's army; we need to encourage one another as the gloom of life sets in. We need to pray one for another as Jesus prayed for Peter that his faith not fail. We need to break the darkness by singing, "Glory, glory, glory." There are more victories to get, more tears to shed, more songs to sing, and more prayers to pray. Until Jesus returns to take us home, we must fight the good fight of faith. One day, we will walk on streets of gold, behold Jesus face-to-face, and sing, "All the way my Savior leads me." I pray to see you there, amen.

Loving Father, we accept your grace and ask you to grant us your peace as we go through the trials of life; you use them to prepare us for our heavenly homes Jesus has gone to prepare for us. We pray He will return soon and we will live in glory now throughout eternity, amen.

Reflections, Thoughts, and Prayer

_____

_____

_____

_____

_____

About the author

Jaël Naomie always had the presence of God in her life, until the Lord became silent. She fasted and prayed for an entire year, but the Lord was still silent. She decided that she would not give up, but her faith was wearing thin. In her feeble spiritual state, she decide to daily pray to God even for just one minute, and all of heaven opened up to her.